HOPE
FOR THE
HUNGRY HEART

HOPE
FOR THE
HUNGRY HEART

Compiled by

Gary Wilde

A
JANET
THOMA
BOOK

Thomas Nelson Publishers
Nashville

Published in Nashville, Tennessee, by Thomas Nelson, Inc., and distributed in Canada by Lawson Falle, Ltd., Cambridge, Ontario.

Scripture quotations are from the NEW KING JAMES VERSION of the Bible. Copyright © 1979, 1980, 1982, Thomas Nelson, Inc., Publishers.

Library of Congress Cataloging-in-Publication Data

Wilde, Gary.
    Hope for the hungry heart : God's promises for overeaters / compiled by Gary Wilde.
        p.   cm. — (New perspectives)
    ISBN 0-8407-3243-0 (pbk.)
    1. Eating disorders—Patients—Prayer-books and devotions—English. I. Title. II. Series.
BV4910.35.W55   1991
242'.4—dc20   92–4025
                                                               CIP
        Printed in the United States of America
            1 2 3 4 5 6 7 — 96 95 94 93 92

CONTENTS

Introduction

Day by day, you're making choices that keep you on the path of recovery from compulsive overeating or food dependency. You are not alone. *Hope for the Hungry Heart* is filled with Scriptures from the New King James Version of the Bible to give you the strength and encouragement you need for every step of your journey. The Scripture verses are arranged topically in chapters according to various stages of recovery.

The first step of any recovery begins with recognizing the problem. And in Part One of this book, you will find verses that help you recognize not only the problem but the need that drives your hunger. As you read through the sections of each chapter, you will be able to ask yourself specific questions relating to your past (What needs have gone unmet in my life?) and to where you are now (Am I anxious? Am I grieving a loss?).

Part Two records the words from Scripture

that help you learn more about who God is, find forgiveness from Him, and see how following His will can lead you to a better way of living. Then in Part Three, you will read God's words about caring for yourself by maintaining healthy physical and spiritual habits.

You may wish to read *Hope for the Hungry Heart* chronologically, meditating on a verse or two every day, following step by step as you identify the needs behind your dependence, turn to God for help, and begin to establish new and healthy patterns of living. Or you may use the book more selectively. On days you are grieving a loss you may turn to the contents page, find the section on grieving, and turn there to meditate on the words of Scripture that relate.

Keep this book beside your bed, or in your briefcase or purse so you can use it throughout the day. And keep your journal nearby to record your thoughts and prayers as you learn more about God and yourself from the Scriptures you read.

Wherever you are in your journey, *Hope for the Hungry Heart* is a companion that offers you words of health and peace.

RECOGNIZING MY HUNGER-NEED

Admitting My Powerlessness Over Food

Just this little bit. Just one more helping. Only a little "cheat." Yet how often has that little nibble developed into a full-fledged binge—starting in motion yet another cycle of guilt-purge-depression . . . and more eating!

How can we break that devastating cycle? We encounter an amazing paradox on the road to recovery: We must give up to get, give over to win over; we must admit defeat before the path to victory opens before us. In the Bible, Jesus said it in so many ways. For instance: "Unless a grain of wheat falls into the ground and dies, it remains alone; but if it dies, it produces much grain" (John 12:24).

When faced with his own failures, ancient Israel's King David lamented, "Like a heavy burden they are too heavy for me" (Ps. 38:4).

Great! For all who echo his words, it's time to lay the burden down.

I Feel Enslaved!

■ *Recognizing My Bondage to Food*

I speak in human terms because of the weakness of your flesh. For just as you presented your members as slaves of uncleanness, and of lawlessness leading to more lawlessness, so now present your members as slaves of righteousness for holiness.

—ROMANS 6:19

By whom a person is overcome, by him also he is brought into bondage.

—2 PETER 2:19

■ *Trying to Cover Up Compulsion*

Lord, all my desire is before You;
And my sighing is not hidden from You.

—PSALM 38:9

There is a way which seems right to a man,
But its end is the way of death.

—PROVERBS 14:12

Do you see a man wise in his own eyes?
There is more hope for a fool than for him.
—PROVERBS 26:12

"Can anyone hide himself in secret places,
So I shall not see him?" says the LORD;
"Do I not fill heaven and earth?" says the
    LORD.

—JEREMIAH 23:24

■ Feeling Weak and Powerless

Have mercy on me, O LORD, for I am weak;
O LORD, heal me, for my bones are troubled.
—PSALM 6:2

"LORD, make me to know my end,
And what is the measure of my days,
That I may know how frail I am.
Indeed, You have made my days as
    handbreadths,
And my age is as nothing before You;
Certainly every man at his best state is but
    vapor."

—PSALM 39:4–5

"Watch and pray, lest you enter into temptation.
The spirit indeed is willing, but the flesh is weak."
—MATTHEW 26:41

■ Suffering Defeat and Discouragement

I am weary with my groaning;
All night I make my bed swim;
I drench my couch with my tears.

PSALM 6:6

How long, O LORD?
Will You forget me forever?
How long will You hide Your face from me?

—PSALM 13:1

My dishonor is continually before me,
And the shame of my face has covered me.

—PSALM 44:15

Reproach has broken my heart,
And I am full of heaviness;
I looked for someone to take pity, but there
    was none;
And for comforters, but I found none.

—PSALM 69:20

For my days are consumed like smoke,
And my bones are burned like a hearth.
My heart is stricken and withered like
    grass, . . .
Because of the sound of my groaning
My bones cling to my skin.

I am like a pelican of the wilderness;
I am like an owl of the desert.
I lie awake,
And am like a sparrow alone on the housetop.

—PSALM 102:3–7

I Admit My Defeat

■ *Struggling in Vain with Willpower*

For I know that in me (that is, in my flesh) nothing good dwells; for to will is present with me, but how to perform what is good I do not find. For the good that I will to do, I do not do; but the evil I will not to do, that I practice. Now if I do what I will not to do, it is no longer I who do it, but sin that dwells in me.

—ROMANS 7:18–20

■ *Letting Go*

The LORD is near to those who have a broken
heart,
And saves such as have a contrite spirit.

—PSALM 34:18

The spirit of a man will sustain him in
    sickness,
But who can bear a broken spirit?
—PROVERBS 18:14

He who trusts in his own heart is a fool,
But whoever walks wisely will be delivered.
—PROVERBS 28:26

■ Giving Up

O LORD, do not rebuke me in Your wrath,
Nor chasten me in Your hot displeasure!
For Your arrows pierce me deeply,
And Your hand presses me down.
There is no soundness in my flesh
Because of Your anger,
Nor is there any health in my bones
Because of my sin.
For my iniquities have gone over my head;
Like a heavy burden they are too heavy for
    me.
My wounds are foul and festering
Because of my foolishness.
I am troubled, I am bowed down greatly;
I go mourning all the day long.
For my loins are full of inflammation,
And there is no soundness in my flesh.

I am feeble and severely broken;
I groan because of the turmoil of my heart.

—PSALM 38:1–8

I Can't Fight This Alone

■ *Recognizing My Limitations*

To You I will cry, O LORD my Rock:
Do not be silent to me,
Lest, if You are silent to me,
I become like those who go down to the pit.

—PSALM 28:1

"Hear, O LORD, and have mercy on me;
LORD, be my helper!"

—PSALM 30:10

■ *Knowing I'm Not Alone*

But You have seen it, for You observe trouble
    and grief,
To repay it by Your hand.
The helpless commits himself to You;
You are the helper of the fatherless.

—PSALM 10:14

In my distress I called upon the LORD,
And cried out to my God;
He heard my voice from His temple,
And my cry came before Him, even to His
    ears.

                           —PSALM 18:6

For I said in my haste,
"I am cut off from before Your eyes";
Nevertheless You heard the voice of my
    supplications
When I cried out to You.

                       —PSALM 31:22

The LORD will command His lovingkindness
    in the daytime,
And in the night His song shall be with me—
A prayer to the God of my life.

                       —PSALM 42:8

Who is weak, and I am not weak?
                   —2 CORINTHIANS 11:29

And He said to me, "My grace is sufficient for
you, for My strength is made perfect in weakness." Therefore most gladly I will rather boast in
my infirmities, that the power of Christ may rest
upon me.

                     —2 CORINTHIANS 12:9

Seeing then that we have a great High Priest who has passed through the heavens, Jesus the Son of God, let us hold fast our confession. For we do not have a High Priest who cannot sympathize with our weaknesses, but was in all points tempted as we are, yet without sin. Let us therefore come boldly to the throne of grace, that we may obtain mercy and find grace to help in time of need.

—HEBREWS 4:14–16

He can have compassion on those who are ignorant and going astray, since he himself is also beset by weakness.

—HEBREWS 5:2

■ Drawing on God's Strength

"Surely you have instructed many,
And you have strengthened weak hands."

—JOB 4:3

He gives power to the weak,
And to those who have no might He increases
   strength.

—ISAIAH 40:29

Likewise the Spirit also helps in our weaknesses. For we do not know what we should pray for as we ought, but the Spirit Himself makes intercession for us with groanings which cannot be uttered.

—ROMANS 8:26

Therefore I take pleasure in infirmities, in reproaches, in needs, in persecutions, in distresses, for Christ's sake. For when I am weak, then I am strong.

—2 CORINTHIANS 12:10

For though He was crucified in weakness, yet He lives by the power of God. For we also are weak in Him, but we shall live with Him by the power of God toward you.

—2 CORINTHIANS 13:4

For we are glad when we are weak and you are strong. And this also we pray, that you may be made complete.

—2 CORINTHIANS 13:9

■ Trusting Christ's Power

On the same day, when evening had come, He said to them, "Let us cross over to the other side." Now when they had left the multitude, they took Him along in the boat as He was. And other little boats were also with Him. And a great windstorm arose, and the waves beat into the boat, so that it was already filling. But He was in the stern, asleep on a pillow. And they awoke Him and said to Him, "Teacher, do You not care that we are perishing?"

Then He arose and rebuked the wind, and said to the sea, "Peace, be still!" And the wind ceased and there was a great calm. But He said to them, "Why are you so fearful? How is it that you have no faith?"

—MARK 4:35–40

Recalling My Childhood Love-Hunger

What was dinnertime like in your family of origin? Pleasant? Calm? Psychologically nurturing? Or was the environment rushed, isolating, swirling with negative messages? Perhaps you came to dislike, even dread, a call to the dinner table.

In some families, eating together meant sharing significant conversation, growing closer together in love and mutual respect. But for many of us, mealtimes never offered that kind of inner satisfaction. If family members actually sat down for a meal together, the point was to get it over with and go on to the next activity. If the event did not include outright squabbling, it usually did require bottling up feelings or avoiding eye contact.

So we ate, but deep needs went unfulfilled. How will we fill them? You've no doubt found that food can dull the pain of that old dinnertime isolation. But it can't fill the gaping void of withheld affection.

As you survey your inner life, consider the questions in this chapter, the biblical illustrations of feelings and circumstances, and the comfort that God and His people can offer. What childhood hungers for love and approval ache for attention? In what ways has overeating provided a way to stuff down that pain—to fill up the love-gap from your past?

What Was Your Mealtime Environment?

■ Anxious Eating

One dies in his full strength,
Being wholly at ease and secure;
Another man dies in the bitterness of his soul,
Never having eaten with pleasure.

—JOB 21:23,25

"Son of man, eat your bread with quaking, and drink your water with trembling and anxiety."

—EZEKIEL 12:18

In the multitude of my anxieties within me,
Your comforts delight my soul.

—PSALM 94:19

There is nothing better for a man than that he
should eat and drink, and that his soul should enjoy good in his labor. This also, I saw, was from
the hand of God.

—ECCLESIASTES 2:24

Every man should eat and drink and enjoy the
good of all his labor—it is the gift of God.

—ECCLESIASTES 3:13

Here is what I have seen: It is good and fitting
for one to eat and drink, and to enjoy the good of
all his labor in which he toils under the sun all the
days of his life which God gives him; for it is his
heritage. As for every man to whom God has
given riches and wealth, and given him power to
eat of it, to receive his heritage and rejoice in his
labor—this is the gift of God.

—ECCLESIASTES 5:18–19

How Much Approval Did You Feel from Your Parents?

■ *Loss of Parental Blessing*

Then it happened, as soon as Isaac had finished blessing Jacob, and Jacob had scarcely gone out from the presence of Isaac his father, that Esau his brother came in from his hunting. He also had made savory food, and brought it to his father, and said to his father, "Let my father arise and eat of his son's game, that your soul may bless me."

And his father Isaac said to him, "Who are you?" And he said, "I am your son, your first-born, Esau."

Then Isaac trembled exceedingly, and said, "Who? Where is the one who hunted game and brought it to me? I ate all of it before you came, and I have blessed him—and indeed he shall be blessed."

When Esau heard the words of his father, he cried with an exceedingly great and bitter cry, and said to his father, . . . "Have you only one blessing, my father? Bless me, even me also, O my father!" And Esau lifted up his voice and wept.

—GENESIS 27:30–34,38

■ *Approval from Your Heavenly Parent*

Go, eat your bread with joy,
And drink your wine with a merry heart;
For God has already accepted your works.

—ECCLESIASTES 9:7

"But in every nation whoever fears Him and works righteousness is accepted by Him."

—ACTS 10:35

He chose us in Him before the foundation of the world that we should be holy and without blame before Him in love, to the praise of the glory of His grace, by which He has made us accepted in the Beloved.

—EPHESIANS 1:4,6

You also, as living stones, are being built up a spiritual house, a holy priesthood, to offer up spiritual sacrifices acceptable to God through Jesus Christ.

—1 PETER 2:5

What Feeling-Needs Went Unsatisfied?

■ *Felt Abandoned, Left Out?*

My God, My God, why have You forsaken Me?

Why are You so far from helping Me,
And from the words of My groaning?
O My God, I cry in the daytime, but You do
not hear;
And in the night season, and am not silent.

—PSALM 22:1–2

"And the younger of them said to his father,
'Father, give me the portion of goods that falls to
me.' So he divided to them his livelihood.

"And not many days after, the younger son
gathered all together, journeyed to a far country,
and there wasted his possessions with prodigal
living. But when he had spent all, there arose a
severe famine in that land, and he began to be in
want. Then he went and joined himself to a citizen
of that country, and he sent him into his fields to
feed swine.

And he would gladly have filled his stomach
with the pods that the swine ate, and no one gave
him anything.

"But when he came to himself, he said, 'How
many of my father's hired servants have bread
enough and to spare, and I perish with hunger! I
will arise and go to my father, and will say to him,
"Father, I have sinned against heaven and before
you, and I am no longer worthy to be called your
son."'"

—LUKE 15:12–19

■ Learning Not to Fear Abandonment

"And he arose and came to his father. But when he was still a great way off, his father saw him and had compassion, and ran and fell on his neck and kissed him."

—LUKE 15:20

"Is not the LORD your God with you? And has He not given you rest on every side?"

—1 CHRONICLES 22:18

For you did not receive the spirit of bondage again to fear, but you received the Spirit of adoption by whom we cry out, "Abba, Father."

—ROMANS 8:15

But now in Christ Jesus you who once were far off have been made near by the blood of Christ.

—EPHESIANS 2:13

■ Felt Uncared for or Abused?

Fathers, do not provoke your children, lest they become discouraged.

—COLOSSIANS 3:21

But if anyone does not provide for his own, and especially for those of his household, he has denied the faith and is worse than an unbeliever.

—1 TIMOTHY 5:8

Yea, though I walk through the valley of the
    shadow of death,
I will fear no evil;
For You are with me;
Your rod and Your staff, they comfort me.

—PSALM 23:4

Sing, O heavens!
Be joyful, O earth!
And break out in singing, O mountains!
For the LORD has comforted His people,
And will have mercy on His afflicted.

—ISAIAH 49:13

"I, even I, am He who comforts you.
Who are you that you should be afraid
Of a man who will die,
And of the son of a man who will be made
    like grass?"

—ISAIAH 51:12

"As one whom his mother comforts,
So I will comfort you;
And you shall be comforted in Jerusalem."

—ISAIAH 66:13

Blessed be the God and Father of our LORD Jesus
Christ, the Father of mercies and God of all com-

fort, who comforts us in all our tribulation, that we may be able to comfort those who are in any trouble, with the comfort with which we ourselves are comforted by God.

—2 CORINTHIANS 1:3–4

■ *Felt Overly Responsible?*

Then Joseph provided his father, his brothers, and all his father's household with bread, according to the number in their families.

—GENESIS 47:12

"So [the older son] answered and said to his father, 'Lo, these many years I have been serving you; I never transgressed your commandment at any time; and yet you never gave me a young goat, that I might make merry with my friends.'"

—LUKE 15:29

But Martha was distracted with much serving, and she approached Him and said, "LORD, do You not care that my sister has left me to serve alone? Therefore tell her to help me."

And Jesus answered and said to her, "Martha, Martha, you are worried and troubled about many things."

—LUKE 10:40–41

■ *Letting God Be Responsible to Provide*

"But one thing is needed, and Mary has chosen that good part, which will not be taken away from her."

—LUKE 10:42

But Isaac spoke to Abraham his father and said, "My father!"

And he said, "Here I am, my son."

And he said, "Look, the fire and the wood, but where is the lamb for a burnt offering?"

And Abraham said, "My son, God will provide for Himself the lamb for a burnt offering." And the two of them went together. And Abraham called the name of the place, The-LORD-Will-Provide; as it is said to this day, "In the Mount of The LORD it shall be provided."

—GENESIS 22:7–8,14

"Who has divided a channel for the
   overflowing water,
Or a path for the thunderbolt,
To cause it to rain on a land where there is no
   one,
A wilderness in which there is no man;
To satisfy the desolate waste,
And cause to spring forth the growth of
   tender grass?

Can you hunt the prey for the lion,
Or satisfy the appetite of the young lions,
When they crouch in their dens,
Or lurk in their lairs to lie in wait?
Who provides food for the raven,
When its young ones cry to God,
And wander about for lack of food?"

—JOB 38:25–27,39–41

You visit the earth and water it,
You greatly enrich it;
The river of God is full of water;
You provide their grain,
For so You have prepared it.

—PSALM 65:9

"Or do you think that I cannot now pray to My Father, and He will provide Me with more than twelve legions of angels?"

—MATTHEW 26:53

Do You Need More Food—Or Reparenting?

■ *Being Reparented by Friends or Relatives*

The women said to Naomi, "Blessed be the LORD, who has not left you this day without a near kinsman."

—RUTH 4:14

A Mother-in-Law Gives Refuge

Orpah kissed her mother-in-law, but Ruth clung to her.

And [Naomi] said, "Look, your sister-in-law has gone back to her people and to her gods; return after your sister-in-law."

But Ruth said:

"Entreat me not to leave you,
Or to turn back from following after you;
For wherever you go, I will go;
And wherever you lodge, I will lodge;
Your people shall be my people,
And your God, my God.
Where you die, I will die,
And there will I be buried.
The LORD do so to me, and more also,
If anything but death parts you and me."

So Naomi returned, and Ruth the Moabitess her daughter-in-law with her, who returned from the country of Moab.

—RUTH 1:14–17,22

A Close Relative Offers Comfort

[Ruth] fell on her face, bowed down to the ground, and said to [Boaz], "Why have I found favor in your eyes, that you should take notice of me, since I am a foreigner?"

And Boaz answered and said to her, "It has been fully reported to me, all that you have done for your mother-in-law since the death of your husband, and how you have left your father and your mother and the land of your birth, and have come to a people whom you did not know before. The LORD repay your work, and a full reward be given you by the LORD God of Israel, under whose wings you have come for refuge."

Then she said, "Let me find favor in your sight, my LORD; for you have comforted me, and have spoken kindly to your maidservant, though I am not like one of your maidservants."

Now Boaz said to her at mealtime, "Come here, and eat of the bread, and dip your piece of bread in the vinegar." So she sat beside the reapers, and he passed parched grain to her; and she ate and was satisfied.

—RUTH 2:10-14

So [Ruth] went down to the threshing floor and did according to all that her mother-in-law instructed her.

And after Boaz had eaten and drunk, and his heart was cheerful, he went to lie down at the end of the heap of grain; and she came softly, uncovered his feet, and lay down. Now it happened at midnight that the man was startled, and turned himself; And [Boaz] said, "Who are you?"

So she answered, "I am Ruth, your maidservant. Take your maidservant under your wing, for you are a near kinsman."

[Boaz said], "And now, my daughter, do not fear. I will do for you all that you request."

—RUTH 3:6–9,11

■ *Being Reparented by God*

A father of the fatherless, a defender of
    widows,
Is God in His holy habitation.

—PSALM 68:5

But now, O LORD,
You are our Father;
We are the clay, and You our potter;
And all we are the work of Your hand.

—ISAIAH 64:8

"As one whom his mother comforts,
So I will comfort you;
And you shall be comforted in Jerusalem."

—ISAIAH 66:13

"Your Father knows the things you have need of before you ask Him."

—MATTHEW 6:8

"If you then, being evil, know how to give good gifts to your children, how much more will your Father who is in heaven give good things to those who ask Him!"

—MATTHEW 7:11

"Are not two sparrows sold for a copper coin? And not one of them falls to the ground apart from your Father's will. You are of more value than many sparrows."

—MATTHEW 10:29,31

"Take heed that you do not despise one of these little ones, for I say to you that in heaven their angels always see the face of My Father who is in heaven. Even so it is not the will of your Father who is in heaven that one of these little ones should perish."

—MATTHEW 18:10,14

"I will be a Father to you,
And you shall be My sons and daughters,
Says the LORD Almighty."

—2 CORINTHIANS 6:18

Behold what manner of love the Father has bestowed on us, that we should be called children of God!

—1 JOHN 3:1

Can You Move Toward Forgiveness?

■ *Forgiving Family Sins of the Past*

So they sent messengers to Joseph, saying, "Before your father died he commanded, saying, 'Thus you shall say to Joseph: "I beg you, please forgive the trespass of your brothers and their sin; for they did evil to you."' Now, please, forgive the trespass of the servants of the God of your father." And Joseph wept when they spoke to him.

Then his brothers also went and fell down before his face, and they said, "Behold, we are your servants."

Joseph said to them, "Do not be afraid, for am I in the place of God? But as for you, you meant evil against me; but God meant it for good. . . ." And he comforted them and spoke kindly to them.

—GENESIS 50:17–21

Then Peter came to Him and said, "LORD, how often shall my brother sin against me, and I forgive him? Up to seven times?" Jesus said to him, "I do not say to you, up to seven times, but up to seventy times seven."

—MATTHEW 18:21–22

"Should you not also have had compassion on your fellow servant, just as I had pity on you?"

—MATTHEW 18:33

Dealing with What's Eating Me

Some psychologists say there are only four basic human emotions: joy, fear, anger, sadness. We may have other feelings, but all of them ultimately derive from one of these Big Four. The anxiety we may feel about an event is closely related to fear, for example.

Our lifestyles betray a suspicion that certain emotions are best avoided—fear, anger sadness. Does that mean that only one emotion is "good"? Though many of us might question such an assumption, we seem to feel it would be better to focus on pleasant, less disturbing things.

One way to avoid fear, anger, and sadness is to go around them. And we can be sustained along our "flight path" by any addiction of our choice (one that usually makes subconscious sense to us, depending on the type of pain from the past that needs dulling). So overeating offers a less disturbing alternative to feeling. It also causes us to miss out on three quarters of our real lives!

Another option is to go through, rather than around, our fear, anger, and sadness. If we choose that route, we will be in for some pain. Yet the Scriptures encourage us: "Those who sow in tears shall reap in joy" (Ps. 126:5). Pleasant surprise! We discover that the Big Four work together. By a full immersion in our pain, we're released to experience the unfathomable depths of our joy.

Am I Anxious?

"My heart is in turmoil and cannot rest;
Days of affliction confront me."

—JOB 30:27

I am feeble and severely broken;
I groan because of the turmoil of my heart.

—PSALM 38:8

My heart wavered, fearfulness frightened me;
The night for which I longed He turned into
  fear for me.

—ISAIAH 21:4

■ Anxiety Due to Worried Rushing and Overwork

So the same day Pharaoh commanded the task-masters of the people their officers, saying, "You shall no longer give the people straw to make brick as before. Let them go and gather straw for themselves. And you shall lay on them the quota of bricks which they made before. You shall not diminish it. . . . Let more work be laid on the men, that they may labor in it. . . ."

And the taskmasters forced them to hurry, saying, "Fulfill your work, your daily quota. . . . Why have you not fulfilled your task in making brick both yesterday and today, as before?"

—EXODUS 5:6–9,13–14

■ Dealing with Worry God's Way

"Do not worry about your life, what you will eat or what you will drink; nor about your body, what you will put on. Is not life more than food and the body more than clothing? Look at the birds of the air, for they neither sow nor reap nor gather into barns; yet your heavenly Father feeds them. Are you not of more value than they? Which of you by worrying can add one cubit to his stature?

"So why do you worry about clothing? Consider the lilies of the field, how they grow: they neither toil nor spin; and yet I say to you that even Solomon in all his glory was not arrayed like one of these. Now if God so clothes the grass of the field, which today is, and tomorrow is thrown into the oven, will He not much more clothe you, O you of little faith? Therefore do not worry, saying, 'What shall we eat?' or 'What shall we drink?' or 'What shall we wear?'

For after all these things the Gentiles seek. For your heavenly Father knows that you need all these things. But seek first the kingdom of God and His righteousness, and all these things shall be added to you. Therefore do not worry about to-morrow, for tomorrow will worry about its own things. Sufficient for the day is its own trouble."

—MATTHEW 6:25–34

■ *Anxiety from Trying to Be Perfect*

"The pride of your heart has deceived you,
You who dwell in the clefts of the rock,
Whose habitation is high;
You who say in your heart,
'Who will bring me down to the ground?'"

—OBADIAH 1:3

Are you so foolish? Having begun in the Spirit, are you now being made perfect by the flesh?

—GALATIANS 3:3

For if anyone thinks himself to be something, when he is nothing, he deceives himself.

—GALATIANS 6:3

For the law, having a shadow of the good things to come, and not the very image of the things, can never with these same sacrifices, which they offer continually year by year, make those who approach perfect.

—HEBREWS 10:1

If we say that we have no sin, we deceive ourselves, and the truth is not in us.

—1 JOHN 1:8

Only God Is Perfect

"He is the Rock, His work is perfect;
For all His ways are justice,
A God of truth and without injustice;
Righteous and upright is He."

—DEUTERONOMY 32:4

"As for God, His way is perfect;
The word of the LORD is proven;
He is a shield to all who trust in Him."

—2 SAMUEL 22:31

Every good gift and every perfect gift is from above, and comes down from the Father of lights, with whom there is no variation or shadow of turning.

—JAMES 1:17

My Perfection Comes from God Alone

"God is my strength and power,
And He makes my way perfect."

—2 SAMUEL 22:33

"Therefore you shall be perfect, just as your Father in heaven is perfect."

—MATTHEW 5:48

Jesus said to him, "If you want to be perfect, go, sell what you have and give to the poor, and you will have treasure in heaven; and come, follow Me."

—MATTHEW 19:21

And He said to me, "My grace is sufficient for you, for My strength is made perfect in weakness." Therefore most gladly I will rather boast in my infirmities, that the power of Christ may rest upon me.

—2 CORINTHIANS 12:9

Him we preach, warning every man and teaching every man in all wisdom, that we may present every man perfect in Christ Jesus.

—COLOSSIANS 1:28

And He Himself gave some to be apostles, some prophets, some evangelists, and some pastors and teachers, for the equipping of the saints for the work of ministry, for the edifying of the body of Christ, till we all come to the unity of the faith and of the knowledge of the Son of God, to a perfect man, to the measure of the stature of the fullness of Christ.

—EPHESIANS 4:11–13

For the law made nothing perfect; on the other hand, there is the bringing in of a better hope, through which we draw near to God.

—HEBREWS 7:19

But may the God of all grace, who called us to His eternal glory by Christ Jesus, after you have suffered a while, perfect, establish, strengthen, and settle you.

—1 PETER 5:10

Am I Fearful?

"Fear came upon me, and trembling,
Which made all my bones shake."

—JOB 4:14

For I hear the slander of many;
Fear is on every side;
While they take counsel together against me,
They scheme to take away my life.

—PSALM 31:13

"But I will show you whom you should fear:
Fear Him who, after He has killed, has power to
cast into hell; yes, I say to you, fear Him!"

—LUKE 12:5

Fearfulness and trembling have come upon
    me,
And horror has overwhelmed me.
And I said, "Oh, that I had wings like a dove!
For then I would fly away and be at rest.
Indeed, I would wander far off,
And remain in the wilderness. Selah
I would hasten my escape
From the windy storm and tempest."

—PSALM 55:5-8

■ Meeting Fear with Divine Courage

"Be strong and of good courage, do not fear nor be afraid of them; for the LORD your God, He is the One who goes with you. He will not leave you nor forsake you."

—DEUTERONOMY 31:6

"Have I not commanded you? Be strong and of good courage; do not be afraid, nor be dismayed, for the LORD your God is with you wherever you go."

—JOSHUA 1:9

Though an army should encamp against me,
My heart shall not fear;
Though war should rise against me,
In this I will be confident.

—PSALM 27:3

Therefore we will not fear,
Though the earth be removed,
And though the mountains be carried into the
  midst of the sea.

—PSALM 46:2

"But whoever listens to me will dwell safely,
And will be secure, without fear of evil."

—PROVERBS 1:33

"Listen to Me, you who know righteousness,
You people in whose heart is My law:
Do not fear the reproach of men,
Nor be afraid of their revilings."

—ISAIAH 51:7

"The very hairs of your head are all numbered. Do not fear therefore; you are of more value than many sparrows."

—LUKE 12:7

"Do not fear, little flock, for it is your Father's good pleasure to give you the kingdom."

—LUKE 12:32

For God has not given us a spirit of fear, but of power and of love and of a sound mind.

—2 TIMOTHY 1:7

There is no fear in love; but perfect love casts out fear, because fear involves torment. But he who fears has not been made perfect in love.

—1 JOHN 4:18

Am I Angry?

Then God saw [the Ninevites'] works, that they turned from their evil way; and God relented from the disaster that He had said He would bring upon them, and He did not do it. But it displeased Jonah exceedingly, and he became angry.

So he prayed to the LORD, . . . "Therefore now, O LORD, please take my life from me, for it is better for me to die than to live!"

Then the LORD said, "Is it right for you to be angry?"

So Jonah went out of the city and sat on the east side of the city. There he made himself a shelter and sat under it in the shade, till he might see what would become of the city. And the LORD God prepared a plant and made it come up over Jonah, that it might be shade for his head to deliver him from his misery. So Jonah was very grateful for the plant. But as morning dawned the next day God prepared a worm, and it so damaged the plant that it withered. And it happened, when the sun arose, that God prepared a vehement east wind; and the sun beat on Jonah's head, so that he grew faint. Then he wished death for himself, and said, "It is better for me to die than to live."

Then God said to Jonah, "Is it right for you to be angry about the plant?"

And he said, "It is right for me to be angry, even to death!"

—JONAH 3:10—4:9

But the LORD said, "You have had pity on the plant for which you have not labored, nor made it grow, which came up in a night and perished in a night. And should I not pity Nineveh, that great city, in which are more than one hundred and twenty thousand persons who cannot discern between their right hand and their left, and also much livestock?"

—JONAH 4:10–11

Be angry, and do not sin.
Meditate within your heart on your bed, and
   be still. Selah

—PSALM 4:4

"But I say to you that whoever is angry with his brother without a cause shall be in danger of the judgment. And whoever says to his brother, 'Raca!' shall be in danger of the council. But whoever says, 'You fool!' shall be in danger of hell fire."

—MATTHEW 5:22

"Be angry, and do not sin": do not let the sun go down on your wrath.

—EPHESIANS 4:26

Let every man be swift to hear, slow to speak, slow to wrath.

—JAMES 1:19

Am I Bitter?

"My soul loathes my life;
I will give free course to my complaint,
I will speak in the bitterness of my soul."

—JOB 10:1

The heart knows its own bitterness,
And a stranger does not share its joy.

—PROVERBS 14:10

Now when Simon saw that through the laying on of the apostles' hands the Holy Spirit was given, he offered them money, saying, "Give me this power also, that anyone on whom I lay hands may receive the Holy Spirit."

But Peter said to him, "Your money perish with you, because you thought that the gift of God could be purchased with money! You have neither part nor portion in this matter, for your heart is not right in the sight of God. Repent therefore of this your wickedness, and pray God if perhaps the thought of your heart may be forgiven you. For I see that you are poisoned by bitterness and bound by iniquity."

—ACTS 8:18–23

■ Curing Bitterness

"You shall not take vengeance, nor bear any grudge against the children of your people, but you shall love your neighbor as yourself: I am the LORD."

—LEVITICUS 19:18

"Indeed it was for my own peace
That I had great bitterness;
But You have lovingly delivered my soul from
   the pit of corruption,
For You have cast all my sins behind Your
   back."

—ISAIAH 38:17

Let all bitterness, wrath, anger, clamor, and evil speaking be put away from you, with all malice.

—EPHESIANS 4:31

[Look] diligently lest anyone fall short of the grace of God; lest any root of bitterness springing

up cause trouble, and by this many become de-
filed.

—HEBREWS 12:15

Have I Sought God's Inner Peace?

"You will keep him in perfect peace,
Whose mind is stayed on You,
Because he trusts in You."

—ISAIAH 26:3

"For he [the man whose hope is in the LORD]
    shall be like a tree planted by the waters,
Which spreads out its roots by the river,
And will not fear when heat comes;
But her leaf will be green,
And will not be anxious in the year of
    drought,
Nor will cease from yielding fruit."

—JEREMIAH 17:8

"Peace I leave with you, My peace I give to you;
not as the world gives do I give to you. Let not
your heart be troubled, neither let it be afraid."

—JOHN 14:27

"These things I have spoken to you, that in Me
you may have peace. In the world you will have

tribulation; but be of good cheer, I have overcome the world."

—JOHN 16:33

For God is not the author of confusion but of peace, as in all the churches of the saints.

—1 CORINTHIANS 14:33

For He Himself is our peace, who has made both one, and has broken down the middle wall of division between us, having abolished in His flesh the enmity, that is, the law of commandments contained in ordinances, so as to create in Himself one new man from the two, thus making peace. And He came and preached peace to you who were afar off and to those who were near.

—EPHESIANS 2:14–15,17

The peace of God, which surpasses all understanding, will guard your hearts and minds through Christ Jesus.

—PHILIPPIANS 4:7

Now may the Lord of peace Himself give you peace always in every way. The Lord be with you all.

—2 THESSALONIANS 3:16

Am I Grieving a Loss?

"Oh, that my grief were fully weighed,
And my calamity laid with it on the scales!"

—JOB 6:2

"Though I speak, my grief is not relieved;
And if I remain silent, how am I eased?"

—JOB 16:6

My eye wastes away because of grief;
It grows old because of all my enemies.

—PSALM 6:7

He is despised and rejected by men,
A Man of sorrows and acquainted with grief.
And we hid, as it were, our faces from Him;
He was despised, and we did not esteem
    Him.
Surely He has borne our griefs
And carried our sorrows;
Yet we esteemed Him stricken,
Smitten by God, and afflicted.
Yet it pleased the LORD to bruise Him;
He has put Him to grief.
When You make His soul an offering for sin,
He shall see His seed,
He shall prolong His days,

And the pleasure of the LORD shall prosper in
    His hand.

—ISAIAH 53:3-4,10

For this is commendable, if because of conscience toward God one endures grief, suffering
wrongfully.

—1 PETER 2:19

■ Seeking God's Comfort in Grief

The LORD had closed [Hannah's] womb . . .
therefore she wept and did not eat. Then Elkanah
her husband said to her, "Hannah, why do you
weep? Why do you not eat? And why is your heart
grieved? Am I not better to you than ten sons?"

So Hannah arose after they had finished eating
and drinking in Shiloh. Now Eli the priest was sitting on the seat by the doorpost of the tabernacle
of the LORD. And she was in bitterness of soul,
and prayed to the LORD and wept in anguish.

"I am a woman of sorrowful spirit [she said to
Eli]. I have drunk neither wine nor intoxicating
drink, but have poured out my soul before the
LORD. Do not consider your maidservant a wicked
woman, for out of the abundance of my complaint
and grief I have spoken until now."

Then Eli answered and said, "Go in peace, and

the God of Israel grant your petition which you
have asked of Him."

And she said, "Let your maidservant find favor
in your sight." So the woman went her way and
ate, and her face was no longer sad.

—1 SAMUEL 1:5,7–10,15–18

"For the LORD has called you
Like a woman forsaken and grieved in spirit,
Like a youthful wife when you were refused,"
Says your God.

—ISAIAH 54:6

Though He causes grief,
Yet He will show compassion
According to the multitude of His mercies.

—LAMENTATIONS 3:32

In this you greatly rejoice, though now for a little while, if need be, you have been grieved by various trials.

—1 PETER 1:6

TURNING TO GOD WITH MY OVEREATING

Confessing My Addiction-Caused Sins Against Others

What can I do? Because of my compulsive and addictive behaviors I have hurt others, either actively or passively. I have withdrawn my emotional life from them.

How can I change? What can I do?

The recovery solution is simple: Do the hardest thing humanly possible. Acknowledge your guilt. Admit your sin. Turn. And sin no more.

We can understand it, of course. But if we didn't have help to do it, it would be impossible, like moving mountains into the sea. No doubt Jesus saw some shocked looks on the faces of those He invited to do just that. He simply reminded them, "With God all things are possible." Even personal transformation, from the inside out.

I Can Respond to God's Call

"Thus says the Lord God: 'Repent, turn away from your idols, and turn your faces away from all your abominations.'"

—EZEKIEL 14:6

Draw near to God and He will draw near to you. Cleanse your hands, you sinners; and purify your hearts, you double-minded.

—JAMES 4:8

■ *I Can Acknowledge My Guilt . . .*

I acknowledged my sin to You,
And my iniquity I have not hidden.
I said, "I will confess my transgressions to the
    Lord,"
And You forgave the iniquity of my sin. Selah

—PSALM 32:5

For I am ready to fall,
And my sorrow is continually before me.
For I will declare my iniquity;
I will be in anguish over my sin.

—PSALM 38:17–18

■ . . . *As David Awakened to His Wrongdoing*

Then the LORD sent Nathan to David. And he came to him, and said to him: "There were two men in one city, one rich and the other poor. The rich man had exceedingly many flocks and herds. But the poor man had nothing, except one little ewe lamb which he had bought and nourished; and it grew up together with him and with his children. It ate of his own food and drank from his own cup and lay in his bosom; and it was like a daughter to him. And a traveler came to the rich man, who refused to take from his own flock and from his own herd to prepare one for the wayfaring man who had come to him; but he took the poor man's lamb and prepared it for the man who had come to him."

Then David's anger was greatly aroused against the man, and he said to Nathan, "As the LORD lives, the man who has done this shall surely die! And he shall restore fourfold for the lamb, because he did this thing and because he had no pity."

Then Nathan said to David, "You are the man!"

Then David said to Nathan, "I have sinned against the LORD."

—2 SAMUEL 12:1–7,13

■ *I May Refuse to Admit Destructive Behaviors . . .*

When I kept silent, my bones grew old
Through my groaning all the day long.
For day and night Your hand was heavy upon
    me;
My vitality was turned into the drought of
    summer.

—PSALM 32:3–4

He who covers his sins will not prosper,
But whoever confesses and forsakes them will
    have mercy.

—PROVERBS 28:13

Happy is the man who is always reverent,
But he who hardens his heart will fall into
    calamity.

—PROVERBS 28:14

■ *. . . But God Sees My Heart*

For the word of God is living and powerful, and
sharper than any two-edged sword, piercing even
to the division of soul and spirit, and of joints and
marrow, and is a discerner of the thoughts and in-
tents of the heart. And there is no creature hidden

from His sight, but all things are naked and open to the eyes of Him to whom we must give account.

—HEBREWS 4:12–13

I Must Forgive, Too

"But I say to you who hear: Love your enemies, do good to those who hate you, bless those who curse you, and pray for those who spitefully use you. To him who strikes you on the one cheek, offer the other also. And from him who takes away your cloak, do not withhold your tunic either. Give to everyone who asks of you. And from him who takes away your goods do not ask them back. And just as you want men to do to you, you also do to them likewise.

"But if you love those who love you, what credit is that to you? For even sinners love those who love them. And if you do good to those who do good to you, what credit is that to you? For even sinners do the same. And if you lend to those from whom you hope to receive back, what credit is that to you? For even sinners lend to sinners to receive as much back. But love your enemies, do good, and lend, hoping for nothing in return; and your reward will be great, and you will be sons of the Highest. For He is kind to the unthankful and evil.

Therefore be merciful, just as your Father also is merciful."

—LUKE 6:27–36

■ *Not Bearing a Grudge*

"Therefore if you bring your gift to the altar, and there remember that your brother has something against you, leave your gift there before the altar, and go your way. First be reconciled to your brother, and then come and offer your gift."

—MATTHEW 5:23–24

■ *Not Hating a "Special Case"*

He who says he is in the light, and hates his brother, is in darkness until now. He who loves his brother abides in the light, and there is no cause for stumbling in him. But he who hates his brother is in darkness and walks in darkness, and does not know where he is going, because the darkness has blinded his eyes.

—1 JOHN 2:9–11

I Can Confess My Sins to Trusted Others

Confess your trespasses to one another, and pray for one another, that you may be healed. The effective, fervent prayer of a righteous man avails much.

—JAMES 5:16

Where there is no counsel, the people fall;
But in the multitude of counselors there is
  safety.

—PROVERBS 11:14

Deceit is in the heart of those who devise evil,
But counselors of peace have joy.

—PROVERBS 12:20

I Can Work for Peace in My Family

Therefore, as the elect of God, holy and beloved, put on tender mercies, kindness, humbleness of mind, meekness, longsuffering; bearing with one another, and forgiving one another, if anyone has a complaint against another; even as Christ forgave you, so you also must do.

—COLOSSIANS 3:12–13

I Can Move from Discord to Love

■ What Is Love?

Though I speak with the tongues of men and of angels, but have not love, I have become as sounding brass or a clanging cymbal. And though I have the gift of prophecy, and understand all mysteries and all knowledge, and though I have all faith, so that I could remove mountains, but have not love, I am nothing. And though I bestow all my goods to feed the poor, and though I give my body to be burned, but have not love, it profits me nothing.

Love suffers long and is kind; love does not envy; love does not parade itself, is not puffed up; does not behave rudely, does not seek its own, is not provoked, thinks no evil; does not rejoice in iniquity, but rejoices in the truth; bears all things, believes all things, hopes all things, endures all things.

Love never fails. But whether there are prophecies, they will fail; whether there are tongues, they will cease; whether there is knowledge, it will vanish away. For we know in part and we prophesy in part. But when that which is perfect has come, then that which is in part will be done away. When I was a child, I spoke as a child, I understood as a child, I thought as a child; but when I became a man, I put away childish things. For now we see in a mirror, dimly, but then face to face. Now I know in part, but then I shall know just as I also am known.

And now abide faith, hope, love, these three; but the greatest of these is love.

—1 CORINTHIANS 13:1–13

■ *How Shall We Love One Another?*

"A new commandment I give to you, that you love one another; as I have loved you. . . . By this all will know that you are My disciples, if you have love for one another."

—JOHN 13:34–35

I Can Watch My Speech Among Those I Love

A soft answer turns away wrath,
But a harsh word stirs up anger.
The tongue of the wise uses knowledge
   rightly,
But the mouth of fools pours forth foolishness.

—PROVERBS 15:1–2

A wholesome tongue is a tree of life,
But perverseness in it breaks the spirit.

—PROVERBS 15:4

He who heeds the word wisely will find good,
And whoever trusts in the LORD, happy is he.

—PROVERBS 16:20

The wise in heart will be called prudent,
And sweetness of the lips increases learning.

—PROVERBS 16:21

Understanding is a wellspring of life to him
   who has it.
But the correction of fools is folly.

—PROVERBS 16:22

The heart of the wise teaches his mouth,
And adds learning to his lips.

—PROVERBS 16:23

Pleasant words are like a honeycomb,
Sweetness to the soul and health to the bones.

—PROVERBS 16:24

A word fitly spoken is like apples of gold
In settings of silver.

—PROVERBS 25:11

Do not speak evil of one another, brethren. He
who speaks evil of a brother and judges his
brother, speaks evil of the law and judges the law.
But if you judge the law, you are not a doer of the
law but a judge.

—JAMES 4:11

I May Still Feel Guilty . . .

Then the scribes and Pharisees brought to
[Jesus] a woman caught in adultery. And when

they had set her in the midst, they said to Him, "Teacher, this woman was caught in adultery, in the very act. Now Moses, in the law, commanded us that such should be stoned. But what do You say?" This they said, testing Him, that they might have something of which to accuse Him.

But Jesus stooped down and wrote on the ground with His finger, as though He did not hear. So when they continued asking Him, He raised Himself up and said to them, "He who is without sin among you, let him throw a stone at her first."

And again He stooped down and wrote on the ground.

Then those who heard it, being convicted by their conscience, went out one by one, beginning with the oldest even to the last. And Jesus was left alone, and the woman standing in the midst.

—JOHN 8:3–9

. . . So I Apply God's Forgiveness

When Jesus had raised Himself up and saw no one but the woman, He said to her, "Woman, where are those accusers of yours? Has no one condemned you?"

She said, "No one, Lord."

And Jesus said to her, "Neither do I condemn you; go and sin no more."

—JOHN 8:10–11

"To the Lord our God belong mercy and forgiveness, though we have rebelled against Him."

—DANIEL 9:9

[David said:]

"Blessed are those whose lawless deeds are
    forgiven
And whose sins are covered.
Blessed is the man to whom the LORD shall
    not impute sin."

—ROMANS 4:7–8

In Him we have redemption through His blood, the forgiveness of sins, according to the riches of His grace.

—EPHESIANS 1:7

And you, being dead in your trespasses and the uncircumcision of your flesh, He has made alive together with Him, having forgiven you all trespasses.

—COLOSSIANS 2:13

If we confess our sins, He is faithful and just to forgive us our sins and to cleanse us from all un-righteousness.

—1 JOHN 1:9

I write to you, little children,
Because your sins are forgiven you for His
name's sake.

—1 JOHN 2:12

Recognizing a Higher Power

Recovery thrusts us into a searching inspection of our lives, causing us to question what they really mean and what we want them to mean in the future. Any time people begin such a search they invariably ask the big questions: What, after all, is the point of my life? Who am I? Where did I come from? Where am I going?

The amazing thing about these questions is where they lead. They push us beyond the confines of our limited, finite horizons—our daily routines, problems, and dreams. We know our lives are finite, because our bodies deteriorate and end up in a grave. Yet the big questions keep leading us beyond the finite. And we secretly know that if any real, satisfying answers are to come, they must come to us from outside our little world of seeing and touching, eating and sleeping. Questions about the meaning of life get us involved in reaching for the infinite. And we come face to face with . . . God.

God Created Me

■ *In the Beginning God Created. . . .*

Then God said, "Let Us make man in Our image, according to Our likeness; let them have dominion over the fish of the sea, over the birds of the air, and over the cattle, over all the earth and over every creeping thing that creeps on the earth."

So God created man in His own image; in the image of God He created him; male and female He created them. Then God blessed them, and God said to them, "Be fruitful and multiply; fill the earth and subdue it; have dominion over the fish of the sea, over the birds of the air, and over every living thing that moves on the earth."

And God said, "See, I have given you every herb that yields seed which is on the face of all the earth, and every tree whose fruit yields seed; to you it shall be for food.

Also, to every beast of the earth, to every bird of the air, and to everything that creeps on the earth, in which there is life, I have given every green herb for food"; and it was so. Then God saw everything that He had made, and indeed it was very good. So the evening and the morning were the sixth day.

—GENESIS 1:1,26–31

God Knows Me Intimately

O LORD, You have searched me and known me.
You know my sitting down and my rising up;
You understand my thought afar off.
You comprehend my path and my lying down,
And are acquainted with all my ways.
For there is not a word on my tongue,
But behold, O LORD, You know it altogether.
You have hedged me behind and before,
And laid Your hand upon me.
Such knowledge is too wonderful for me;
It is high, I cannot attain it.
Where can I go from Your Spirit?
Or where can I flee from Your presence?
If I ascend into heaven, You are there;
If I make my bed in hell, behold, You are there.
If I take the wings of the morning,
And dwell in the uttermost parts of the sea,

Even there Your hand shall lead me,
And Your right hand shall hold me.
If I say, "Surely the darkness shall fall on me,"
Even the night shall be light about me;
Indeed, the darkness shall not hide from You,
But the night shines as the day;
The darkness and the light are both alike to
    You.
For You formed my inward parts;
You covered me in my mother's womb.
I will praise You, for I am fearfully and
    wonderfully made;
Marvelous are Your works,
And that my soul knows very well.
My frame was not hidden from You,
When I was made in secret,
And skillfully wrought in the lowest parts of
    the earth.
Your eyes saw my substance, being yet
    unformed.
And in Your book they all were written,
The days fashioned for me,
When as yet there were none of them.
                                    —PSALM 139:1–16

"But the very hairs of your head are all
    numbered."

                                    —MATTHEW 10:30

God Cares for Me
As My Shepherd

The LORD is my shepherd;
I shall not want.
He makes me to lie down in green pastures;
He leads me beside the still waters.
He restores my soul;
He leads me in the paths of righteousness
For His name's sake.
Yea, though I walk through the valley of the
    shadow of death,
I will fear no evil;
For You are with me;
Your rod and Your staff, they comfort me.
You prepare a table before me in the presence
    of my enemies;
You anoint my head with oil;
My cup runs over.
Surely goodness and mercy shall follow me
All the days of my life;
And I will dwell in the house of the LORD
Forever.

—PSALM 23:1–6

■ As My Strength and Protector

The LORD is my strength and my shield;
My heart trusted in Him, and I am helped;

Therefore my heart greatly rejoices,
And with my song I will praise Him.
The LORD is their strength,
And He is the saving refuge of His anointed.

—PSALM 28:7–8

Hear my cry, O God;
Attend to my prayer.
From the end of the earth I will cry to You,
When my heart is overwhelmed;
Lead me to the rock that is higher than I.
For You have been a shelter for me,
A strong tower from the enemy.
I will abide in Your tabernacle forever;
I will trust in the shelter of Your wings. Selah

—PSALM 61:1–4

My soul, wait silently for God alone,
For my expectation is from Him.
He only is my rock and my salvation;
He is my defense;
I shall not be moved.
In God is my salvation and my glory;
The rock of my strength,
And my refuge, is in God.

—PSALM 62:5–7

He who dwells in the secret place of the Most
   High

Shall abide under the shadow of the Almighty.
I will say of the LORD, "He is my refuge and
   my fortress;
My God, in Him I will trust."
Surely He shall deliver you from the snare of
   the fowler
And from the perilous pestilence.
He shall cover you with His feathers,
And under His wings you shall take refuge;
His truth shall be your shield and buckler.

—PSALM 91:1-4

■ As My Guide Through Life

I will instruct you and teach you in the way
   you should go;
I will guide you with My eye.

—PSALM 32:8

For this is God,
Our God forever and ever;
He will be our guide
Even to death.

—PSALM 48:14

Trust in the LORD with all your heart,
And lean not on your own understanding;
In all your ways acknowledge Him,
And He shall direct your paths.

—PROVERBS 3:5-6

Your ears shall hear a word behind you,
    saying,
"This is the way, walk in it,"
Whenever you turn to the right hand
Or whenever you turn to the left.

—ISAIAH 30:21

■ As My Courage-Giver

Whenever I am afraid,
I will trust in You.
In God (I will praise His word),
In God I have put my trust;
I will not fear.
What can flesh do to me?

—PSALM 56:3–4

■ As My Refuge

God is our refuge and strength,
A very present help in trouble.
Therefore we will not fear,
Though the earth be removed,
And though the mountains be carried into the
midst of the sea; Though its waters roar and be
troubled,
Though the mountains shake with its swelling.
Selah

—PSALM 46:1–3

In You, O LORD, I put my trust;
Let me never be put to shame.
Deliver me in Your righteousness, and cause
me to escape;
Incline Your ear to me, and save me.
Be my strong habitation,
To which I may resort continually;
You have given the commandment to save me,
For You are my rock and my fortress.

—PSALM 71:1–3

God Is Wonderful to Know

■ *He Is Close*

Then Paul stood in the midst of the Areopagus
and said, "Men of Athens, I perceive that in all
things you are very religious; for as I was passing
through and considering the objects of your worship, I even found an altar with this inscription:
TO THE UNKNOWN GOD.

"Therefore, the One whom you worship without knowing, Him I proclaim to you: God, who
made the world and everything in it, since He is
Lord of heaven and earth, does not dwell in tem-
ples made with hands. Nor is He worshiped with
men's hands, as though He needed anything,
since He gives to all life, breath, and all things.

And He has made from one blood every nation of men to dwell on all the face of the earth, and has determined their preappointed times and the boundaries of their habitation, so that they should seek the Lord, in the hope that they might grope for Him and find Him, though He is not far from each one of us; for in Him we live and move and have our being, as also some of your own poets have said, 'For we are also His offspring.'

"Therefore, since we are the offspring of God, we ought not to think that the Divine Nature is like gold or silver or stone, something shaped by art and man's devising. Truly, these times of ignorance God overlooked, but now commands all men everywhere to repent."

—ACTS 17:22–30

■ He Is Good

Oh, how great is Your goodness,
Which You have laid up for those who fear
     You,
Which You have prepared for those who trust
     in You
In the presence of the sons of men!
You shall hide them in the secret place of Your
     presence
From the plots of man;

You shall keep them secretly in a pavilion
From the strife of tongues.

—PSALM 31:19–20

Oh, that men would give thanks to the LORD
   for His goodness,
And for His wonderful works to the children
   of men!

—PSALM 107:31

■ *He Is Loving*

Yet He sets the poor on high, far from
   affliction,
And makes their families like a flock.
The righteous see it and rejoice,
And all iniquity stops its mouth.
Whoever is wise will observe these things,
And they will understand the lovingkindness
   of the LORD.

—PSALM 107:41–43

For I am persuaded that neither death nor life,
nor angels nor principalities nor powers, nor
things present nor things to come, nor height nor
depth, nor any other created thing, shall be able to
separate us from the love of God which is in Christ
Jesus our Lord.

—ROMANS 8:38–39

■ *He Is Merciful*

Be merciful to me, O God, be merciful to
    me!
For my soul trusts in You;
And in the shadow of Your wings I will make
    my refuge,
Until these calamities have passed by.
He shall send from heaven and save me;
He reproaches the one who would swallow
    me up. Selah
God shall send forth His mercy and His
    truth.
For Your mercy reaches unto the heavens,
And Your truth unto the clouds.

—PSALM 57:1,3,10

My merciful God shall come to meet me;
God shall let me see my desire on my
    enemies.
But I will sing of Your power;
Yes, I will sing aloud of Your mercy in the
    morning;
For You have been my defense
And refuge in the day of my trouble.
To You, O my Strength, I will sing praises;
For God is my defense,
The God of my mercy.

—PSALM 59:10,16,17

Also to You, O Lord, belongs mercy;
For You render to each one according to his
    work.

—PSALM 62:12

Oh, do not remember former iniquities against
    us!
Let Your tender mercies come speedily to meet
    us,
For we have been brought very low.

—PSALM 79:8

For You, Lord, are good, and ready to forgive,
And abundant in mercy to all those who call
    upon You.

—PSALM 86:5

If I say, "My foot slips,"
Your mercy, O LORD, will hold me up.

—PSALM 94:18

For the LORD is good;
His mercy is everlasting,
And His truth endures to all generations.

—PSALM 100:5

■ He Saves Me

The LORD is my rock and my fortress and my
    deliverer;

My God, my strength, in whom I will trust;
My shield and the horn of my salvation, my
  stronghold.
I will call upon the LORD, who is worthy to be
  praised;
So shall I be saved from my enemies.

—PSALM 18:2–3

■ He Gives Good Gifts

And He said to them, "Which of you shall have
a friend, and go to him at midnight and say to
him, 'Friend, lend me three loaves; for a friend of
mine has come to me on his journey, and I have
nothing to set before him'; and he will answer
from within and say, 'Do not trouble me; the door
is now shut, and my children are with me in bed; I
cannot rise and give to you'? I say to you, though
he will not rise and give to him because he is his
friend, yet because of his persistence he will rise
and give him as many as he needs.

"And I say to you, ask, and it will be given to
you; seek, and you will find; knock, and it will be
opened to you. For everyone who asks receives,
and he who seeks finds, and to him who knocks it
will be opened.

"If a son asks for bread from any father among
you, will he give him a stone? Or if he asks for a
fish, will he give him a serpent instead of a fish?

Or if he asks for an egg, will he offer him a scorpion? If you then, being evil, know how to give good gifts to your children, how much more will your heavenly Father give the Holy Spirit to those who ask Him!"

—LUKE 11:5-13

■ *He Restores to Wholeness*

Now He was teaching in one of the synagogues on the Sabbath. And behold, there was a woman who had a spirit of infirmity eighteen years, and was bent over and could in no way raise herself up. But when Jesus saw her, He called her to Him and said to her, "Woman, you are loosed from your infirmity." And He laid His hands on her, and immediately she was made straight, and glorified God.

—LUKE 13:10–13

God Can Be Fully Known Through His Son

"And this is eternal life, that they may know You, the only true God, and Jesus Christ whom You have sent."

—JOHN 17:3

■ Jesus Made Unique Claims

I Am the Bread of Life

And Jesus said to them, "I am the bread of life. He who comes to Me shall never hunger, and he who believes in Me shall never thirst. But I said to you that you have seen Me and yet do not believe. All that the Father gives Me will come to Me, and the one who comes to Me I will by no means cast out. For I have come down from heaven, not to do My own will, but the will of Him who sent Me. This is the will of the Father who sent Me, that of all He has given Me I should lose nothing, but should raise it up at the last day. And this is the will of Him who sent Me, that everyone who sees the Son and believes in Him may have everlasting life; and I will raise him up at the last day."

—JOHN 6:35-40

I Am the Light of the World

Then Jesus spoke to them again, saying, "I am the light of the world. He who follows Me shall not walk in darkness, but have the light of life."

The Pharisees therefore said to Him, "You bear witness of Yourself; Your witness is not true."

Jesus answered and said to them, "Even if I bear

witness of Myself, My witness is true, for I know where I came from and where I am going; but you do not know where I come from and where I am going."

—JOHN 8:12–14

I Am the Door and the Good Shepherd

Then Jesus said to them again, "Most assuredly, I say to you, I am the door of the sheep. All who ever came before Me are thieves and robbers, but the sheep did not hear them.

I am the door. If anyone enters by Me, he will be saved, and will go in and out and find pasture. The thief does not come except to steal, and to kill, and to destroy. I have come that they may have life, and that they may have it more abundantly.

"I am the good shepherd. The good shepherd gives His life for the sheep. But he who is a hireling and not the shepherd, one who does not own the sheep, sees the wolf coming and leaves the sheep and flees; and the wolf catches the sheep and scatters them. The hireling flees because he is a hireling and does not care about the sheep.

"I am the good shepherd; and I know My sheep, and am known by My own. As the Father knows Me, even so I know the Father; and I lay down My life for the sheep. And other sheep I have which are not of this fold; them also I must

bring, and they will hear My voice; and there will
be one flock and one shepherd."

—JOHN 10:7–16

I Am the Resurrection and the Life

Then Martha said to Jesus, "Lord, if You had
been here, my brother would not have died. But
even now I know that whatever You ask of God,
God will give You."

Jesus said to her, "Your brother will rise again."

Martha said to Him, "I know that he will rise
again in the resurrection at the last day."

Jesus said to her, "I am the resurrection and the
life. He who believes in Me, though he may die, he
shall live. And whoever lives and believes in Me
shall never die. Do you believe this?"

—JOHN 11:21–26

I Am One with the Father

Then the Jews surrounded Him and said to
Him, "How long do You keep us in doubt? If You
are the Christ, tell us plainly."

Jesus answered them, "I told you, and you do
not believe. The works that I do in My Father's
name, they bear witness of Me. But you do not believe, because you are not of My sheep, as I said to
you. My sheep hear My voice, and I know them,
and they follow Me. And I give them eternal life,

and they shall never perish; neither shall anyone snatch them out of My hand. My Father, who has given them to Me, is greater than all; and no one is able to snatch them out of My Father's hand. I and My Father are one."

Then the Jews took up stones again to stone Him.

Jesus answered them, "Many good works I have shown you from My Father. For which of those works do you stone Me?"

The Jews answered Him, saying, "For a good work we do not stone You, but for blasphemy, and because You, being a Man, make Yourself God."

Jesus answered them, "Is it not written in your law, 'I said, "You are gods"'? If He called them gods, to whom the word of God came (and the Scripture cannot be broken), do you say of Him whom the Father sanctified and sent into the world, 'You are blaspheming,' because I said, 'I am the Son of God'? If I do not do the works of My Father, do not believe Me; but if I do, though you do not believe Me, believe the works, that you may know and believe that the Father is in Me, and I in Him."

—JOHN 10:24–38

I Am the Vine

"I am the true vine, and My Father is the vinedresser.

Every branch in Me that does not bear fruit He takes away; and every branch that bears fruit He prunes, that it may bear more fruit. You are already clean because of the word which I have spoken to you. Abide in Me, and I in you. As the branch cannot bear fruit of itself, unless it abides in the vine, neither can you, unless you abide in Me. "I am the vine, you are the branches. He who abides in Me, and I in him, bears much fruit; for without Me you can do nothing. If anyone does not abide in Me, he is cast out as a branch and is withered; and they gather them and throw them into the fire, and they are burned. If you abide in Me, and My words abide in you, you will ask what you desire, and it shall be done for you."

—JOHN 15:1–7

I Am the Only Way to God

Jesus said to [Thomas], "I am the way, the truth, and the life. No one comes to the Father except through Me."

—JOHN 14:6

[Peter said,] "Nor is there salvation in any other, for there is no other name under heaven given among men by which we must be saved."

—ACTS 4:12

For He made Him who knew no sin to be sin for us, that we might become the righteousness of God in Him.

—2 CORINTHIANS 5:21

[Jesus] gave Himself for our sins, that He might deliver us from this present evil age, according to the will of our God and Father.

—GALATIANS 1:4

■ Jesus Shared Our Human Nature

Inasmuch then as the children have partaken of flesh and blood, He Himself likewise shared in the same, that through death He might destroy him who had the power of death, that is, the devil, and release those who through fear of death were all their lifetime subject to bondage. For indeed He does not give aid to angels, but He does give aid to the seed of Abraham. Therefore, in all things He had to be made like His brethren, that He might be a merciful and faithful High Priest in things pertaining to God, to make propitiation for the sins of the people. For in that He Himself has suffered, being tempted, He is able to aid those who are tempted.

—HEBREWS 2:14-18

■ *Jesus Bore Our Sins*

[Jesus] Himself bore our sins in His own body on the tree, that we, having died to sins, might live for righteousness—by whose stripes you were healed. For you were like sheep going astray, but have now returned to the Shepherd and Overseer of your souls.

—1 PETER 2:24–25

Turning My Will Over to God

Ever been lost in the woods? It can be pretty scary to realize you've been walking in circles—with the food and water running out.

For many of us, the idea of turning our wills over to God seems like an invitation to enter blindly into the most threatening wilderness. What loss of control! Giving up the power to make life's directional choices; letting go of the life-and-career-planning reins. How will I survive if I don't keep grabbing what I need for myself? Yet the woman entered the wilderness and she was fed for 1,260 days (see Rev. 12:6)!

Turn it over to God. He will provide. The apostle Paul put it like this: "Now may He who supplies seed to the sower, and bread for food, supply and multiply the seed you have sown and increase the fruits of your righteousness, while you are enriched in everything" (2 Cor. 9:10–11).

Seeking a Better Way to Live

If you cry out for discernment,
And lift up your voice for understanding,
If you seek her as silver,
And search for her as for hidden treasures;
Then you will understand the fear of the
   LORD,
And find the knowledge of God.
For the LORD gives wisdom;
From His mouth come knowledge and
   understanding;
He stores up sound wisdom for the upright;
He is a shield to those who walk uprightly.

—PROVERBS 2:3–7

"For My thoughts are not your thoughts,
Nor are your ways My ways," says the LORD.
"For as the heavens are higher than the earth,
So are My ways higher than your ways,
And My thoughts than your thoughts."

—ISAIAH 55:8–9

■ *Crying Out to God* . . .

Help me, O LORD my God!
Oh, save me according to Your mercy.

—PSALM 109:26

Out of the depths I have cried to You, O
    LORD;
Lord, hear my voice!
Let Your ears be attentive
To the voice of my supplications.
If You, LORD, should mark iniquities,
O Lord, who could stand?
But there is forgiveness with you,
That you may be feared.
I wait for the LORD, my soul waits,
And in His word I do hope.
My soul waits for the Lord
More than those who watch for the morning—
Yes, more than those who watch for the
    morning.

—PSALM 130:1–6

I cry out to the LORD with my voice;
With my voice to the LORD I make my
    supplication.
I pour out my complaint before Him;
I declare before Him my trouble.
When my spirit was overwhelmed within me,

Then You knew my path.
In the way in which I walk
They have secretly set a snare for me.
Look on my right hand and see,
For there is no one who acknowledges me;
Refuge has failed me;
No one cares for my soul.
I cried out to You, O Lord:
I said, "You are my refuge,
My portion in the land of the living.
Attend to my cry,
For I am brought very low;
Deliver me from my persecutors,
For they are stronger than I."

—PSALM 142:1–6

■ . . . Results in "Seeing" and Following Him

Now as they departed from Jericho, a great multitude followed Him. And behold, two blind men sitting by the road, when they heard that Jesus was passing by, cried out, saying,

"Have mercy on us, O Lord, Son of David!"

Then the multitude warned them that they should be quiet; but they cried out all the more, saying, "Have mercy on us, O Lord, Son of David!"

So Jesus stood still and called them, and said, "What do you want Me to do for you?"

They said to Him, "Lord, that our eyes may be opened."

So Jesus had compassion and touched their eyes. And immediately their eyes received sight, and they followed Him.

—MATTHEW 20:29–34

I love the LORD, because He has heard
My voice and my supplications.
Because He has inclined His ear to me,
Therefore I will call upon Him as long as I
     live.

—PSALM 116:1–2

Understanding God's Offer of New Life

■ It Is Responding to Christ's Call

"Come to Me, all you who labor and are heavy laden, and I will give you rest. Take My yoke upon you and learn from Me, for I am gentle and lowly in heart, and you will find rest for your souls. For My yoke is easy and My burden is light."

—MATTHEW 11:28–30

On the last day, that great day of the feast, Jesus stood and cried out, saying, "If anyone thirsts, let him come to Me and drink. He who believes in

Me, as the Scripture has said, out of his heart will flow rivers of living water."

—JOHN 7:37–38

■ *It Is God's Work from the Beginning*

He chose us in Him before the foundation of the world, that we should be holy and without blame before Him in love, having predestined us to adoption as sons by Jesus Christ to Himself, according to the good pleasure of His will, to the praise of the glory of His grace, by which He has made us accepted in the Beloved. In Him we have redemption through His blood, the forgiveness of sins, according to the riches of His grace which He made to abound toward us in all wisdom and prudence, having made known to us the mystery of His will, according to His good pleasure which He purposed in Himself, that in the dispensation of the fullness of the times He might gather together in one all things in Christ, both which are in heaven and which are on earth—in Him, in whom also we have obtained an inheritance, being predestined according to the purpose of Him who works all things according to the counsel of His will, that we who first trusted in Christ should be to the praise of His glory. In Him you also trusted, after you heard the word of truth, the gospel of your salvation; in whom also, having believed, you were sealed with the Holy Spirit of promise, who is the guarantee of our inheritance until the redemption of the purchased possession, to the praise of His glory.

—EPHESIANS 1:4–14

■ *It Is Not by Works, but by Grace*

For by grace you have been saved through faith, and that not of yourselves; it is the gift of God, not of works, lest anyone should boast.

—EPHESIANS 2:8–9

But now the righteousness of God apart from the law is revealed, being witnessed by the Law and the Prophets, even the righteousness of God, which is through faith in Jesus Christ, to all and on all who believe. For there is no difference; for all have sinned and fall short of the glory of God, being justified freely by His grace through the redemption that is in Christ Jesus.

—ROMANS 3:21–24

Therefore, having been justified by faith, we have peace with God through our Lord Jesus Christ.

—ROMANS 5:1

But God demonstrates His own love toward us, in that while we were still sinners, Christ died for us. Much more then, having now been justified by His blood, we shall be saved from wrath through Him. For if when we were enemies we were reconciled to God through the death of His Son, much more, having been reconciled, we shall be saved by His life.

And not only that, but we also rejoice in God through our Lord Jesus Christ, through whom we have now received the reconciliation.

—ROMANS 5:8–11

Believing

■ Just Call on God and Believe

If you confess with your mouth the Lord Jesus and believe in your heart that God has raised Him from the dead, you will be saved. For with the heart one believes to righteousness, and with the mouth confession is made to salvation. For the Scripture says, "Whoever believes on Him will not be put to shame." For there is no distinction between Jew and Greek, for the same Lord over all is rich to all who call upon Him. For "whoever calls on the name of the LORD shall be saved."

—ROMANS 10:9–13

While He was still speaking, some came from the ruler of the synagogue's house who said, "Your daughter is dead. Why trouble the Teacher any further?"

As soon as Jesus heard the word that was spoken, He said to the ruler of the synagogue, "Do not be afraid; only believe."

—MARK 5:35–36

Jesus said to him, "If you can believe, all things are possible to him who believes."

Immediately the father of the child cried out and said with tears, "Lord, I believe; help my unbelief!"

—MARK 9:23–24

Enjoying the Results of Belief

But as many as received Him, to them He gave the right to become children of God, even to those who believe in His name: who were born, not of blood, nor of the will of the flesh, nor of the will of man, but of God.

—JOHN 1:12–13

"Most assuredly, I say to you, he who hears My word and believes in Him who sent Me has everlasting life, and shall not come into judgment, but has passed from death into life."

—JOHN 5:24

There is therefore now no condemnation to those who are in Christ Jesus, who do not walk according to the flesh, but according to the Spirit.

—ROMANS 8:1

But now Christ is risen from the dead, and has become the firstfruits of those who have fallen asleep. For since by man came death, by Man also came the resurrection of the dead. For as in Adam all die, even so in Christ all shall be made alive.

—1 CORINTHIANS 15:20–22

And you, being dead in your trespasses and the uncircumcision of your flesh, He has made alive together with Him, having forgiven you all trespasses, having wiped out the handwriting of requirements that was against us, which was contrary to us. And He has taken it out of the way, having nailed it to the cross.

—COLOSSIANS 2:13–14

Blessed be the God and Father of our Lord Jesus Christ, who according to His abundant mercy has begotten us again to a living hope through the resurrection of Jesus Christ from the dead, to an inheritance incorruptible and undefiled and that does not fade away, reserved in heaven for you, who are kept by the power of God through faith for salvation ready to be revealed in the last time.

—1 PETER 1:3–5

Taking Up the Challenge of a God-Centered Life

■ *Giving Up My Life*

"He who loves father or mother more than Me is not worthy of Me. And he who loves son or daughter more than Me is not worthy of Me. And he who does not take his cross and follow after Me is not worthy of Me. He who finds his life will lose it, and he who loses his life for My sake will find it."

—MATTHEW 10:37–39

■ *Looking to God Daily*

So He said to them, "When you pray, say:
Our Father in heaven,
Hallowed be Your name.
Your kingdom come.
Your will be done

On earth as it is in heaven.
Give us day by day our daily bread.
And forgive us our sins,
For we also forgive everyone who is indebted
  to us.
And do not lead us into temptation,
But deliver us from the evil one."

—LUKE 11:2–4

■ *Following Without Looking Back*

Now it happened as they journeyed on the road, that someone said to Him, "Lord, I will follow You wherever You go."

And Jesus said to him, "Foxes have holes and birds of the air have nests, but the Son of Man has nowhere to lay His head."

Then He said to another, "Follow Me."

But he said, "Lord, let me first go and bury my father."

Jesus said to him, "Let the dead bury their own dead, but you go and preach the kingdom of God."

And another also said, "Lord, I will follow You, but let me first go and bid them farewell who are at my house."

But Jesus said to him, "No one, having put his hand to the plow, and looking back, is fit for the kingdom of God."

—LUKE 9:57–62

Giving Up Overeating

It's tough to fight intense craving, especially the desire for something so comforting as food. It seems the harder we try to maintain balanced eating, the more frustrating our failures can be. We weigh ourselves and then agree with the little girl's words to her playmate, as she pointed to the bathroom scales: "All I know is you stand on it and it makes you angry."

But God does respond to our perseverance. A woman came to Jesus once with intense desire that her daughter be healed. Jesus initially tested her desire by putting her off. When she persisted, however, He said, "Let it be to you as you desire" (Matt. 15:28).

So desire, intense craving, can be a good thing. If your desire is to give up your addiction and live in the freedom of God's desires for you, then keep craving.

Being Willing to "Suffer"

Let this mind be in you which was also in Christ
Jesus, who, being in the form of God, did not consider it robbery to be equal with God, but made
Himself of no reputation, taking the form of a
bondservant, and coming in the likeness of men.
And being found in appearance as a man, He
humbled Himself and became obedient to the
point of death, even the death of the cross.

—PHILIPPIANS 2:5-8

Therefore, my beloved, as you have always
obeyed, not as in my presence only, but now much
more in my absence, work out your own salvation
with fear and trembling.

—PHILIPPIANS 2:12

■ Willing to Forego the "Pleasure" of an Addiction

He who loves pleasure will be a poor man;
He who loves wine and oil will not be rich.

—PROVERBS 21:17

I said in my heart, "Come now, I will test you
with mirth; therefore enjoy pleasure"; but surely,
this also was vanity.

—ECCLESIASTES 2:1

But she who lives in pleasure is dead while she lives.

—1 TIMOTHY 5:6

But know this, that in the last days perilous times will come: For men will be lovers of themselves, lovers of money, boasters, proud, blasphemers, disobedient to parents, unthankful, unholy, unloving, unforgiving, slanderers, without self-control, brutal, despisers of good, traitors, headstrong, haughty, lovers of pleasure rather than lovers of God.

—2 TIMOTHY 3:1–4

For the grace of God that brings salvation has appeared to all men, teaching us that, denying ungodliness and worldly lusts, we should live soberly, righteously, and godly in the present age, looking for the blessed hope and glorious appearing of our great God and Savior Jesus Christ, who gave Himself for us, that He might redeem us from every lawless deed and purify for Himself His own special people, zealous for good works.

—TITUS 2:11–14

Where do wars and fights come from among you? Do they not come from your desires for pleasure that war in your members?

—JAMES 4:1

You have lived on the earth in pleasure and lux-
ury; you have fattened your hearts as in a day of
slaughter.

—JAMES 5:5

[False teachers] will receive the wages of unrigh-
teousness, as those who count it pleasure to ca-
rouse in the daytime. They are spots and
blemishes, carousing in their own deceptions
while they feast with you.

—2 PETER 2:13

■ Putting to Death Former Desires

Therefore put to death your members which are
on the earth: fornication, uncleanness, passion,
evil desire, and covetousness, which is idolatry.
Because of these things the wrath of God is coming upon the sons of disobedience, in which you
yourselves once walked when you lived in them.

—COLOSSIANS 3:5–7

Therefore gird up the loins of your mind, be sober, and rest your hope fully upon the grace that is
to be brought to you at the revelation of Jesus
Christ; as obedient children, not conforming yourselves to the former lusts, as in your ignorance;
but as He who called you is holy, you also be holy

in all your conduct, because it is written, "Be holy, for I am holy."

—1 PETER 1:13–16

■ *Turning Away from the "Worthless"*

Remove from me the way of lying,
And grant me Your law graciously.
I have chosen the way of truth;
Your judgments I have laid before me.
I cling to Your testimonies;
O LORD, do not put me to shame!
I will run in the way of Your commandments,
For You shall enlarge my heart.
Teach me, O LORD, the way of Your statutes,
And I shall keep it to the end.
Give me understanding, and I shall keep Your
  law; Indeed, I shall observe it with my
  whole heart.
Make me walk in the path of Your
  commandments,
For I delight in it.
Incline my heart to Your testimonies,
And not to covetousness.
Turn away my eyes from looking at worthless
  things,
And revive me in Your way.

—PSALM 119:29–37

■ Submitting to God's Discipline

And you have forgotten the exhortation which speaks to you as to sons:

My son, do not despise the chastening of the LORD,

Nor be discouraged when you are rebuked by Him;

For whom the LORD loves He chastens,

And scourges every son whom He receives."

If you endure chastening, God deals with you as with sons; for what son is there whom a father does not chasten?

But if you are without chastening, of which all have become partakers, then you are illegitimate and not sons. Furthermore, we have had human fathers who corrected us, and we paid them respect. Shall we not much more readily be in subjection to the Father of spirits and live? For they indeed for a few days chastened us as seemed best to them, but He for our profit, that we may be partakers of His holiness.

Now no chastening seems to be joyful for the present, but grievous; nevertheless, afterward it yields the peaceable fruit of righteousness to those who have been trained by it.

—HEBREWS 12:5–11

But He gives more grace. Therefore He says:
"God resists the proud,
But gives grace to the humble."

—JAMES 4:6

Abiding in Christ to Keep from Overeating

Whoever commits sin also commits lawless-ness, and sin is lawlessness. And you know that He was manifested to take away our sins, and in Him there is no sin. Whoever abides in Him does not sin. Whoever sins has neither seen Him nor known Him. Little children, let no one deceive you. He who practices righteousness is righteous, just as He is righteous. He who sins is of the devil, for the devil has sinned from the beginning. For this purpose the Son of God was manifested, that He might destroy the works of the devil. Whoever has been born of God does not sin, for His seed remains in him; and he cannot sin, because he has been born of God.

—1 JOHN 3:4–9

■ *Giving Up Old Ways*

What shall we say then? Shall we continue in sin that grace may abound? Certainly not! How shall we who died to sin live any longer in it? Or do you not know that as many of us as were baptized into Christ Jesus were baptized into His death? Therefore we were buried with Him through baptism into death, that just as Christ was raised from the dead by the glory of the Father, even so we also should walk in newness of life.

Likewise you also, reckon yourselves to be dead indeed to sin, but alive to God in Christ Jesus our Lord.

Therefore do not let sin reign in your mortal body, that you should obey it in its lusts.

—ROMANS 6:1–4, 11–12

■ Walking in a New Way

I say then: Walk in the Spirit, and you shall not fulfill the lust of the flesh. For the flesh lusts against the Spirit, and the Spirit against the flesh; and these are contrary to one another, so that you do not do the things that you wish.

—GALATIANS 5:16–17

This I say, therefore, and testify in the Lord, that you should no longer walk as the rest of the Gentiles walk, in the futility of their mind, having their understanding darkened, being alienated from the life of God, because of the ignorance that is in them, because of the hardening of their heart; who, being past feeling, have given themselves over to licentiousness, to work all uncleanness with greediness. But you have not so learned Christ, if indeed you have heard Him and have been taught by Him, as the truth is in Jesus: that you put off, concerning your former conduct, the old man which grows corrupt according to the deceitful lusts, and be renewed in the spirit of your mind.

—EPHESIANS 4:17–23

For you were once darkness, but now you are light in the Lord. Walk as children of light (for the fruit of the Spirit is in all goodness, righteousness, and truth), proving what is acceptable to the Lord.

—EPHESIANS 5:8–10

■ Maintaining an Attitude of Humility

LORD, You have heard the desire of the
    humble;
You will prepare their heart;
You will cause Your ear to hear.

—PSALM 10:17

Good and upright is the LORD;
Therefore He teaches sinners in the way.
The humble He guides in justice,
And the humble He teaches His way.

For Your name's sake, O LORD,
Pardon my iniquity, for it is great.

—PSALM 25:8–9,11

Before destruction the heart of a man is
   haughty,
And before honor is humility.

—PROVERBS 18:12

By humility and the fear of the LORD
Are riches and honor and life.

—PROVERBS 22:4

At that time the disciples came to Jesus, saying, "Who then is greatest in the kingdom of heaven?"

And Jesus called a little child to Him, set him in the midst of them, and said, "Assuredly, I say to you, unless you are converted and become as little children, you will by no means enter the kingdom of heaven. Therefore whoever humbles himself as this little child is the greatest in the kingdom of heaven."

—MATTHEW 18:1–4

Also He spoke this parable to some who trusted in themselves that they were righteous, and despised others:

"Two men went up to the temple to pray, one a Pharisee and the other a tax collector. The Pharisee stood and prayed thus with himself, 'God, I thank You that I am not like other men—extortioners, unjust, adulterers, or even as this tax collector. I fast twice a week; I give tithes of all that I possess.'

"And the tax collector, standing afar off, would not so much as raise his eyes to heaven, but beat his breast, saying, 'God, be merciful to me a sinner!'

"I tell you, this man went down to his house justified rather than the other; for everyone who exalts himself will be abased, and he who humbles himself will be exalted."

—LUKE 18:9–14

Therefore humble yourselves under the mighty hand of God, that He may exalt you in due time.

—1 PETER 5:6

Believing That God Responds to Perseverance

And behold, a woman of Canaan came from that region and cried out to Him, saying, "Have mercy on me, O Lord, Son of David! My daughter is severely demon-possessed."

But He answered her not a word. And His disciples came and urged Him, saying, "Send her away, for she cries out after us."

But He answered and said, "I was not sent except to the lost sheep of the house of Israel."

Then she came and worshiped Him, saying, "Lord, help me!"

But He answered and said, "It is not good to take the children's bread and throw it to the little dogs."

And she said, "True, Lord, yet even the little dogs eat the crumbs which fall from their masters' table."

Then Jesus answered and said to her, "O woman, great is your faith! Let it be to you as you desire." And her daughter was healed from that very hour.

—MATTHEW 15:22–28

MAINTAINING MY HUNGER-SATISFIED LIFE

Valuing More than Food

Where is food on your scale of priorities? Writer Richard Foster said: "The person who does not seek the Kingdom first, does not seek it at all, regardless of how worthy the idolatry that he or she has substituted for it."

Consider some of the classic "idols" (substitutes for the Kingdom) found in this chapter: physical appearance, respectability, success, possessions, pleasure (and, of course, food). The trouble with almost every idol is that it is a good thing, overly valued. If life consists of a constant reshuffling of priorities and restructuring of values, then we are open to idolatry at every turn. But those in recovery know that sanity can be maintained only by keeping one value permanently etched at the top of the list: God and His Kingdom.

Food Is a Gift from God

Then the whole congregation of the children of Israel murmured against Moses and Aaron in the wilderness. And the children of Israel said to them, "Oh, that we had died by the hand of the LORD in the land of Egypt, when we sat by the pots of meat and when we ate bread to the full! For you have brought us out into this wilderness to kill this whole assembly with hunger."

Then the LORD said to Moses, "Behold, I will rain bread from heaven for you. . . . Speak to [the children of Israel] saying, 'At twilight you shall eat meat, and in the morning you shall be filled with bread. And you shall know that I am the LORD your God.'"

And the children of Israel ate manna forty years, until they came to an inhabited land; they ate manna until they came to the border of the land of Canaan.

—EXODUS 16:2–4,12,35

All wait for You,
That You may give them their food in due
season.

—PSALM 104:27

Oh, give thanks to the LORD, for He is good!
For His mercy endures forever.

Who gives food to all flesh,
For His mercy endures forever.

—PSALM 136:1,25

The eyes of all look expectantly to You,
And You give them their food in due season.

—PSALM 145:15

Life Is More than Food

■ *More than Enough Food Can Still Be Unsatisfying*

Now the mixed multitude who were among them yielded to intense craving; so the children of Israel also wept again and said: "Who will give us meat to eat? We remember the fish which we ate freely in Egypt, the cucumbers, the melons, the leeks, the onions, and the garlic; but now our whole being is dried up; there is nothing at all except this manna before our eyes!"

Now Moses heard the people weeping throughout their families, everyone at the door of his tent; and the anger of the LORD was greatly aroused; Moses also was displeased.

[The Lord said to Moses], "Then you shall say to

the people, 'Sanctify yourselves for tomorrow, and you shall eat meat; for you have wept in the hearing of the LORD, saying, "Who will give us meat to eat? For it was well with us in Egypt!" Therefore the LORD will give you meat, and you shall eat. You shall eat, not one day, nor two days, nor five days, nor ten days, nor twenty days, but for a whole month, until it comes out of your nostrils and becomes loathsome to you, because you have despised the LORD who is among you.'" . . .

Now a wind went out from the LORD, and it brought quail from the sea and left them fluttering near the camp, about a day's journey on this side and about a day's journey on the other side, all around the camp, and about two cubits above the surface of the ground. And the people stayed up all that day, all that night, and all the next day, and gathered the quail (he who gathered least gathered ten homers); and they spread them out for themselves all around the camp. But while the meat was still between their teeth, before it was chewed, the wrath of the LORD was aroused against the people, and the LORD struck the people with a very great plague. So he called the name of that place Kibroth Hattaavah, because there they buried the people who had yielded to craving.

—NUMBERS 11:4–6,10,18–20,31–34

■ *Food Can Overshadow the Spiritual Life*

Then He spoke a parable to them, saying: "The ground of a certain rich man yielded plentifully. And he thought within himself, saying, 'What shall I do, since I have no room to store my crops?' So he said, 'I will do this: I will pull down my barns and build greater, and there I will store all my crops and my goods. And I will say to my soul, "Soul, you have many goods laid up for many years; take your ease; eat, drink, and be merry."'

"But God said to him, 'You fool! This night your soul will be required of you; then whose will those things be which you have provided?'

"So is he who lays up treasure for himself, and is not rich toward God."

—LUKE 12:16–21

"Life is more than food."

—LUKE 12:23

What I Dwell on Shows My True Values

■ *Dwelling on Things of Finite Value*

You make his beauty melt away like a moth;
Surely every man is vapor. Selah

—PSALM 39:11

"All flesh is grass,
And all its loveliness is like the flower of the
field."

—ISAIAH 40:6

For what is your life? It is even a vapor that appears for a little time and then vanishes away.

—JAMES 4:14

■ Dwelling on Things of Infinite Value

Jesus said to him, "You shall love the LORD your God with all your heart, with all your soul, and with all your mind."

—MATTHEW 22:37

And do not be conformed to this world, but be transformed by the renewing of your mind, that you may prove what is that good and acceptable and perfect will of God.

For I say, through the grace given to me, to everyone who is among you, not to think of himself more highly than he ought to think, but to think soberly, as God has dealt to each one a measure of faith.

—ROMANS 12:2–3

And be renewed in the spirit of your mind.

—EPHESIANS 4:23

Finally, brethren, whatever things are true, whatever things are noble, whatever things are just, whatever things are pure, whatever things are lovely, whatever things are of good report, if there is any virtue and if there is anything praiseworthy—meditate on these things.

—PHILIPPIANS 4:8

Set your mind on things above, not on things on the earth.

—COLOSSIANS 3:2

"For this is the covenant that I will make with the house of Israel: After those days," says the LORD: "I will put My laws in their mind and write them on their hearts; and I will be their God, and they shall be My people."

—HEBREWS 8:10

Therefore gird up the loins of your mind, be sober, and rest your hope fully upon the grace that is to be brought to you at the revelation of Jesus Christ.

—1 PETER 1:13

Life's Meaning: More than External Appearances

■ *Not Just Physical Beauty*

The LORD said to Samuel, . . . "For the LORD does not see as man sees; for man looks at the outward appearance, but the LORD looks at the heart."

—1 SAMUEL 16:7

Do you look at things according to the outward appearance? If anyone is convinced in himself that he is Christ's, let him again consider this in himself, that just as he is Christ's, even so we are Christ's.

—2 CORINTHIANS 10:7

Absalom's Beautiful Hair . . .

Now in all Israel there was no one who was praised as much as Absalom for his good looks. From the sole of his foot to the crown of his head there was no blemish in him. And when he cut the hair of his head—at the end of every year he cut it because it was heavy on him—when he cut it, he weighed the hair of his head at two hundred shekels according to the king's standard.

—2 SAMUEL 14:25–26

For the battle there was scattered over the face of the whole countryside, and the woods devoured more people that day than the sword devoured.

Then Absalom met the servants of David. Absalom rode on a mule. The mule went under the thick boughs of a great terebinth tree, and his head caught in the terebinth; so he was left hanging between heaven and earth. And the mule which was under him went on.

Now a certain man saw it and told Joab, and said, "I just saw Absalom hanging in a terebinth tree!"

So Joab said to the man who told him, "You just saw him! And why did you not strike him there to the ground? I would have given you ten shekels of silver and a belt."

But the man said to Joab, "Though I were to receive a thousand shekels of silver in my hand, I would not raise my hand against the king's son. For in our hearing the king commanded you and Abishai and Ittai, saying, 'Beware lest anyone touch the young man Absalom!' Otherwise I would have dealt falsely against my own life. For there is nothing hidden from the king, and you yourself would have set yourself against me."

Then Joab said, "I cannot linger with you." And

he took three spears in his hand and thrust them through Absalom's heart, while he was still alive in the midst of the terebinth tree.

—2 SAMUEL 18:8–14

■ Not Just Stature

For the message of the cross is foolishness to those who are perishing, but to us who are being saved it is the power of God. For it is written:

"I will destroy the wisdom of the wise

And bring to nothing the understanding of the prudent."

Where is the wise? Where is the scribe? Where is the disputer of this age? Has not God made foolish the wisdom of this world? For since, in the wisdom of God, the world through wisdom did not know God, it pleased God through the foolishness of the message preached to save those who believe.

For you see your calling, brethren, that not many wise according to the flesh, not many mighty, not many noble, are called. But God has chosen the foolish things of the world to put to shame the wise, and God has chosen the weak things of the world to put to shame the things which are mighty; and the base things of the world and the things which are despised God has chosen, and the things which are not, to bring to nothing the things that are, that no flesh should glory in His presence.

—1 CORINTHIANS 1:18–21,26–29

Let no one deceive himself. If anyone among you seems to be wise in this age, let him become a fool that he may become wise. For the wisdom of this world is foolishness with God. For it is written, "He catches the wise in their own craftiness."

—1 CORINTHIANS 3:18–19

We are fools for Christ's sake.

—1 CORINTHIANS 4:10

Life's Goal: Christ Manifested in My Body

But we have this treasure in earthen vessels, that the excellence of the power may be of God and not of us. We are hard pressed on every side, yet not crushed; we are perplexed, but not in despair; persecuted, but not forsaken; struck down, but not destroyed—always carrying about in the body the dying of the Lord Jesus, that the life of Jesus also may be manifested in our body. For we who live are always delivered to death for Jesus' sake, that the life of Jesus also may be manifested in our mortal flesh.

—2 CORINTHIANS 4:7–11

Therefore, if anyone is in Christ, he is a new creation; old things have passed away; behold, all things have become new.

—2 CORINTHIANS 5:17

God's Values Confront Worldly Values

Then Jesus was led up by the Spirit into the wilderness to be tempted by the devil. And when He had fasted forty days and forty nights, afterward He was hungry. Now when the tempter came to Him, he said, "If You are the Son of God, command that these stones become bread."

But He answered and said, "It is written, 'Man shall not live by bread alone, but by every word that proceeds from the mouth of God.'"

Again, the devil took Him up on an exceedingly high mountain, and showed Him all the kingdoms of the world and their glory. And he said to Him, "All these things I will give You if You will fall down and worship me."

Then Jesus said to him, "Away with you, Satan! For it is written, 'You shall worship the LORD your God, and Him only you shall serve.'"

Then the devil left Him, and behold, angels came and ministered to Him.

—MATTHEW 4:1–4,8–11

"For what is a man profited if he gains the whole world, and loses his own soul? Or what will a man give in exchange for his soul?"

—MATTHEW 16:26

"He who loves his life will lose it, and he who hates his life in this world will keep it for eternal life."

—JOHN 12:25

But God forbid that I should glory except in the cross of our Lord Jesus Christ, by whom the world has been crucified to me, and I to the world.

—GALATIANS 6:14

Therefore, if you died with Christ from the basic principles of the world, why, as though living in the world, do you subject yourselves to regulations?

—COLOSSIANS 2:20

Do not love the world or the things in the world. If anyone loves the world, the love of the Father is not in him. For all that is in the world—the lust of the flesh, the lust of the eyes, and the pride of life—is not of the Father but is of the world. And the world is passing away, and the lust of it; but he who does the will of God abides forever.

—1 JOHN 2:15–17

For whatever is born of God overcomes the world. And this is the victory that has overcome the world—our faith.

Who is he who overcomes the world, but he who believes that Jesus is the Son of God?

—1 JOHN 5:4–5

For many deceivers have gone out into the world who do not confess Jesus Christ as coming in the flesh. This is a deceiver and an antichrist.

—2 JOHN 1:7

Then the seventh angel sounded: And there were loud voices in heaven, saying, "The kingdoms of this world have become the kingdoms of our Lord and of His Christ, and He shall reign forever and ever!"

—REVELATION 11:5

It's Okay to Be Hungry

Not that I speak in regard to need, for I have learned in whatever state I am, to be content: I know how to be abased, and I know how to abound. Everywhere and in all things I have learned both to be full and to be hungry. . . . I can do all things through Christ who strengthens me.

—PHILIPPIANS 4:11–13

Taking Care of Myself— While Eating Right

As children we may often have wondered: Who will take care of me? Someone (usually) responded with varying degrees of care and concern. Yet we keep asking the question throughout our adult lives until we finally come up with the somewhat unsettling answer: I am the only one who is really going to take care of me! If I don't do it (including staying in touch with my Higher Power), then no one else will.

At first this revelation can be quite shocking. But recovery persons take up the challenge and begin to do the things that will bring them comfort, nurture, healing—whatever they need to stay on track.

Getting Beyond My Shame

My dishonor is continually before me,
And the shame of my face has covered me.

—PSALM 44:15

You know my reproach, my shame, and my
    dishonor;
My adversaries are all before You.

—PSALM 69:19

In You, O LORD, I put my trust;
Let me never be put to shame.

—PSALM 71:1

"Do not fear, for you will not be ashamed;
Nor be disgraced, for you will not be put to
    shame;
For you will forget the shame of your youth."

—ISAIAH 54:4

Instead of your shame you shall have double
    honor,
And instead of confusion they shall rejoice in
    their portion.
Therefore in their land they shall possess
    double;
Everlasting joy shall be theirs.

—ISAIAH 61:7

"You shall eat in plenty and be satisfied,
And praise the name of the LORD your God,
Who has dealt wondrously with you;
And My people shall never be put to shame.
Then you shall know that I am in the midst of
    Israel,
And that I am the LORD your God
And there is no other.
My people shall never be put to shame."

—JOEL 2:26–27

As it is written:
"Behold, I lay in Zion a stumbling stone and
    rock of offense,
And whoever believes on Him will not be put
    to shame."

—ROMANS 9:33

Looking unto Jesus, the author and finisher of
our faith, who for the joy that was set before Him
endured the cross, despising the shame, and has
sat down at the right hand of the throne of God.

—HEBREWS 12:2

Meeting My Nurture Needs

■ *Clearly Voicing My Needs*

And so it was, when they had crossed over, that
Elijah said to Elisha, "Ask! What may I do for you,
before I am taken away from you?"

And Elisha said, "Please let a double portion of your spirit be upon me."

—2 KINGS 2:9

"'Ask of Me, and I will give You
The nations for Your inheritance,
And the ends of the earth for Your
    possession.'"

—PSALM 2:8

Thus says the LORD:
"Stand in the ways and see,
And ask for the old paths, where the good
    way is,
And walk in it;
Then you will find rest for your souls."

—JEREMIAH 6:16

Ask the LORD for rain
In the time of the latter rain.
The LORD will make flashing clouds;
He will give them showers of rain,
Grass in the field for everyone.

—ZECHARIAH 10:1

"For your Father knows the things you have need of before you ask Him."

—MATTHEW 6:8

"Again I say to you that if two of you agree on earth concerning anything that they ask, it will be done for them by My Father in heaven."

—MATTHEW 18:19

"And all things, whatever you ask in prayer, believing, you will receive."

—MATTHEW 21:22

"If you abide in Me, and My words abide in you, you will ask what you desire, and it shall be done for you."

—JOHN 15:7

"Until now you have asked nothing in My name. Ask, and you will receive, that your joy may be full."

—JOHN 16:24

Now to Him who is able to do exceedingly abundantly above all that we ask or think, according to the power that works in us, to Him be glory.

—EPHESIANS 3:20–21

And whatever we ask we receive from Him, because we keep His commandments and do those things that are pleasing in His sight.

—1 JOHN 3:22

Now this is the confidence that we have in Him, that if we ask anything according to His will, He hears us. And if we know that He hears us, whatever we ask, we know that we have the petitions that we have asked of Him.

—1 JOHN 5:14–15

■ *Making Time for Myself*

So He Himself often withdrew into the wilderness and prayed.

—LUKE 5:16

Walk in wisdom toward those who are outside, redeeming the time.

—COLOSSIANS 4:5

You do not know what will happen tomorrow. For what is your life? It is even a vapor that appears for a little time and then vanishes away.

—JAMES 4:14

To Rest and Refresh

Then the Lord appeared to [Abraham] by the terebinth trees of Mamre, as he was sitting in the tent door in the heat of the day. So he lifted his eyes and looked, and behold, three men were standing by him; and when he saw them, he ran from the tent door to meet them, and bowed himself to the ground, and said, "My Lord, if I have now found favor in Your sight, do not pass on by Your servant. Please let a little water be brought and wash your feet, and rest yourselves under the tree. "And I will bring a morsel of bread, that you may refresh your hearts. After that you may pass by, inasmuch as you have come to your servant."

—GENESIS 18:1–5

"Six days you shall do your work, and on the seventh day you shall rest."

—EXODUS 23:12

Now when He got into a boat, His disciples followed Him. And suddenly a great tempest arose on the sea, so that the boat was covered with the waves. But He was asleep.

—MATTHEW 8:23–24

Then the apostles gathered to Jesus and told Him all things, both what they had done and what they had taught.

And He said to them, "Come aside by yourselves to a deserted place and rest a while." For there were many coming and going, and they did not even have time to eat. So they departed to a deserted place in the boat by themselves.

—MARK 6:30–32

To Meditate and Learn

But when it pleased God, who separated me from my mother's womb and called me through His grace, to reveal His Son in me, that I might preach Him among the Gentiles, I did not immediately confer with flesh and blood, nor did I go up to Jerusalem to those who were apostles before me; but I went to Arabia, and returned again to Damascus. Then after three years I went up to Jerusalem to see Peter, and remained with him fifteen days.

—GALATIANS 1:15–18

■ *Staying Healthy through Exercise and Physical Maintenance*

For by You I can run against a troop;
By my God I can leap over a wall.

—2 SAMUEL 22:30

He gives power to the weak,
And to those who have no might He increases
    strength.
Even the youths shall faint and be weary,
And the young men shall utterly fall,
But those who wait on the LORD
Shall renew their strength;
They shall mount up with wings like eagles,

They shall run and not be weary,
They shall walk and not faint.

—ISAIAH 40:29–31

"For I will restore health to you
And heal you of your wounds," says the
    LORD.

—JEREMIAH 30:17

"But to you who fear My name
The Sun of Righteousness shall arise
With healing in His wings."

—MALACHI 4:2

I beseech you therefore, brethren, by the mercies of God, that you present your bodies a living sacrifice, holy, acceptable to God, which is your reasonable service.

—ROMANS 12:1

Or do you not know that your body is the temple of the Holy Spirit who is in you, whom you have from God, and you are not your own? For you were bought at a price; therefore glorify God in your body and in your spirit, which are God's.

—1 CORINTHIANS 6:19–20

For our citizenship is in heaven, from which we also eagerly wait for the Savior, the Lord Jesus

Christ, who will transform our lowly body that it may be conformed to His glorious body, according to the working by which He is able even to subdue all things to Himself.

—PHILIPPIANS 3:20–21

■ *Finding Comfort Through Friends and Other Christians*

A friend loves at all times,
And a brother is born for adversity.

—PROVERBS 17:17

Be kindly affectionate to one another with brotherly love, in honor giving preference to one another.

—ROMANS 12:10

I thank my God . . . for your fellowship in the gospel from the first day until now.

—PHILIPPIANS 1:3,5

Therefore comfort each other and edify one another, just as you also are doing.

—1 THESSALONIANS 5:11

Now we exhort you, brethren, warn those who are unruly, comfort the fainthearted, uphold the weak, be patient with all.

—1 THESSALONIANS 5:14

And let us consider one another in order to stir up love and good works, not forsaking the assembling of ourselves together, as is the manner of some, but exhorting one another, and so much the more as you see the Day approaching.

—HEBREWS 10:24–25

And the prayer of faith will save the sick, and the Lord will raise him up. And if he has committed sins, he will be forgiven.

—JAMES 5:15

If we say that we have fellowship with Him, and walk in darkness, we lie and do not practice the truth. But if we walk in the light as He is in the light, we have fellowship with one another, and the blood of Jesus Christ His Son cleanses us from all sin.

—1 JOHN 1:6–7

Maintaining Positive Self-Esteem by Resting in God's Validation

■ *Who Am I? . . .*

Now Moses kept the flock of Jethro his father-in-law, the priest of Midian. And he led the flock to the back of the desert, and came to Horeb, the mountain of God. And the Angel of the LORD appeared to him in a flame of fire from the midst of a bush. So he looked, and behold, the bush was burning with fire, but the bush was not consumed. Then Moses said, "I will now turn aside and see this great sight, why the bush does not burn."

So when the LORD saw that he turned aside to look, God called to him from the midst of the bush and said, "Moses, Moses!"

And he said, "Here I am."

Then He said, "Do not draw near this place. Take your sandals off your feet, for the place where you stand is holy ground." Moreover He said, "I am the God of your father—the God of Abraham, the God of Isaac, and the God of Jacob." And Moses hid his face, for he was afraid to look upon God.

"Come now, therefore, and I will send you to Pharaoh that you may bring My people, the children of Israel, out of Egypt."

But Moses said to God, "Who am I . . . ?"

—EXODUS 3:1–6, 10–11

■ . . . I am a Treasure, a Pearl, a Great Catch!

"Then the righteous will shine forth as the sun in the kingdom of their Father. He who has ears to hear, let him hear!

"Again the kingdom of heaven is like treasure hidden in a field, which a man found and hid; and for joy over it he goes and sells all that he has and buys that field.

"Again, the kingdom of heaven is like a merchant seeking beautiful pearls, who, when he had found one pearl of great price, went and sold all that he had and bought it.

"Again, the kingdom of heaven is like a dragnet that was cast into the sea and gathered some of every kind, which, when it was full, they drew to shore; and they sat down and gathered the good into vessels, but threw the bad away. So it will be at the end of the age. The angels will come forth, separate the wicked from among the just.

—MATTHEW 13:43–50

Looking to the Future, Rather than Dwelling on the Past

The LORD is your keeper;
The LORD is your shade at your right hand.
The sun shall not strike you by day,
Nor the moon by night.
The LORD shall preserve you from all evil;
He shall preserve your soul.

The LORD shall preserve your going out and
   your coming in
From this time forth, and even forevermore.
—PSALM 121:5–8

For I know the thoughts that I think toward you,
says the LORD, thoughts of peace and not of evil,
to give you a future and a hope.
—JEREMIAH 29:11

"However, when He, the Spirit of truth, has
come, He will guide you into all truth; for He will
not speak on His own authority, but whatever He
hears He will speak; and He will tell you things to
come."
—JOHN 16:13

Continuing My New, Healthy Habits

And when [Paul and Barnabas] had preached
the gospel to that city and made many disciples,
they returned to Lystra, Iconium, and Antioch,
strengthening the souls of the disciples, exhorting
them to continue in the faith, and saying, "We
must through many tribulations enter the kingdom of God."
—ACTS 14:21–22

Therefore consider the goodness and severity of God: on those who fell, severity; but toward you, goodness, if you continue in His goodness. Otherwise you also will be cut off.

—ROMANS 11:22

But what I do, I will also continue to do, that I may cut off the opportunity from those who desire an opportunity to be regarded just as we are in the things of which they boast.

—2 CORINTHIANS 11:12

And you, who once were alienated and enemies in your mind by wicked works, yet now He has reconciled in the body of His flesh through death, to present you holy, and blameless, and irreproachable in His sight—if indeed you continue in the faith, grounded and steadfast, and are not moved away from the hope of the gospel which you heard.

—COLOSSIANS 1:21-23

Therefore we also, since we are surrounded by so great a cloud of witnesses, let us lay aside every weight, and the sin which so easily ensnares us, and let us run with endurance the race that is set before us.

—HEBREWS 12:1

Take heed to yourself and to the doctrine. Continue in them, for in doing this you will save both yourself and those who hear you.

—1 TIMOTHY 4:16

But as for you, continue in the things which you have learned and been assured of, knowing from whom you have learned them.

—2 TIMOTHY 3:14

Sticking to My Diet Plans

It takes heroic action to deal with temptation, to stick it out, to endure in the face of
an old habit's compelling allure. Emerson once
said, "A man is a hero, not because he is
braver than anyone else, but because he is
brave for ten minutes longer." If we do resist,
we do it one moment at a time, as each choice
comes our way.

The Scripture promises that God is at our
side, minute by minute. It only remains for us
to recognize Him and call upon Him for
strength.

Dealing with Temptation

Let no one say when he is tempted, "I am
tempted by God"; for God cannot be tempted by
evil, nor does He Himself tempt anyone. But each

one is tempted when he is drawn away by his own desires and enticed.

—JAMES 1:13–14

■ *I Must Withstand It*

Be strong in the Lord and in the power of His might.

Put on the whole armor of God, that you may be able to stand against the wiles of the devil. For we do not wrestle against flesh and blood, but against principalities, against powers, against the rulers of the darkness of this age, against spiritual hosts of wickedness in the heavenly places.

Therefore take up the whole armor of God, that you may be able to withstand in the evil day, and having done all, to stand. Stand therefore, having girded your waist with truth, having put on the breastplate of righteousness, and having shod your feet with the preparation of the gospel of peace; above all, taking the shield of faith with which you will be able to quench all the fiery darts of the wicked one. And take the helmet of salvation, and the sword of the Spirit, which is the word of God; praying always with all prayer and supplication in the Spirit, being watchful to this end with all perseverance and supplication for all the saints.

—EPHESIANS 6:10–18

But the Lord is faithful, who will establish you and guard you from the evil one.

—2 THESSALONIANS 3:3

■ *I Must Confront the Tempter*

Then Jesus, being filled with the Holy Spirit, returned from the Jordan and was led by the Spirit into the wilderness.

And the devil said to Him, "If You are the Son of God, command this stone to become bread."

But Jesus answered him, saying, "It is written, 'Man shall not live by bread alone, but by every word of God.'"

Then the devil, taking Him up on a high mountain, showed Him all the kingdoms of the world in a moment of time. And the devil said to Him, "All this authority I will give You, and their glory; for this has been delivered to me, and I give it to whomever I wish. Therefore, if You will worship before me, all will be Yours."

And Jesus answered and said to him, "Get behind Me, Satan! For it is written, 'You shall worship the LORD your God, and Him only you shall serve.'"

Then he brought Him to Jerusalem, set Him on the pinnacle of the temple, and said to Him, "If You are the Son of God, throw Yourself down from here. For it is written:

'He shall give His angels charge over You,
To keep you,'
"and,
'In their hands they shall bear You up,
Lest You dash Your foot against a stone.'"
And Jesus answered and said to him, "It has been said, 'You shall not tempt the LORD your God.'"
Now when the devil had ended every temptation, he departed from Him until an opportune time.

—LUKE 4:1,3–13

Be sober, be vigilant; because your adversary the devil walks about like a roaring lion, seeking whom he may devour.

Resist him, steadfast in the faith, knowing that the same sufferings are experienced by your brotherhood in the world.

But may the God of all grace, who called us to His eternal glory by Christ Jesus, after you have suffered a while, perfect, establish, strengthen, and settle you.

—1 PETER 5:8–10

■ God Understands My Weakness

The LORD is merciful and gracious,
Slow to anger, and abounding in mercy.

He will not always strive with us,
Nor will He keep His anger forever.
He has not dealt with us according to our
   sins,
Nor punished us according to our iniquities.
For as the heavens are high above the earth,
So great is His mercy toward those who fear
   Him;
As far as the east is from the west,
So far has He removed our transgressions
   from us.
As a father pities his children,
So the LORD pities those who fear Him.
For He knows our frame;
He remembers that we are dust.

—PSALM 103:8–14

No temptation has overtaken you except such as is common to man; but God is faithful, who will not allow you to be tempted beyond what you are able, but with the temptation will also make the way of escape, that you may be able to bear it.

—1 CORINTHIANS 10:13

■ Jesus Prays for Me

"I pray for them. I do not pray for the world but for those whom You have given Me, for they are Yours. And all Mine are Yours, and Yours are

Mine, and I am glorified in them. Now I am no longer in the world, but these are in the world, and I come to You. Holy Father, keep through Your name those whom You have given Me, that they may be one as We are. While I was with them in the world, I kept them in Your name. Those whom You gave Me I have kept; and none of them is lost except the son of perdition, that the Scripture might be fulfilled.

"But now I come to You, and these things I speak in the world, that they may have My joy fulfilled in themselves. I have given them Your word; and the world has hated them because they are not of the world, just as I am not of the world. I do not pray that You should take them out of the world, but that You should keep them from the evil one."

—JOHN 17:9–15

Dealing with Relapse

But now after you have known God, or rather are known by God, how is it that you turn again to the weak and beggarly elements, to which you desire again to be in bondage? Stand fast therefore in the liberty by which Christ has made us free, and do not be entangled again with a yoke of bondage.

For you, brethren, have been called to liberty; only do not use liberty as an opportunity for the flesh, but through love serve one another.

—GALATIANS 4:9; 5:1,13

■ Peter First Failed . . .

Now Peter sat outside in the courtyard. And a servant girl came to him, saying, "You also were with Jesus of Galilee."

But he denied it before them all, saying, "I do not know what you are saying."

And when he had gone out to the gateway, another girl saw him and said to those who were there, "This fellow also was with Jesus of Nazareth."

But again he denied with an oath, "I do not know the Man!"

And after a while those who stood by came up and said to Peter, "Surely you also are one of them, for your speech betrays you."

Then he began to curse and swear, saying, "I do not know the Man!"

Immediately a rooster crowed. And Peter remembered the word of Jesus who had said to him, "Before the rooster crows, you will deny Me three times." So he went out and wept bitterly.

—MATTHEW 26:69–75

[Jesus] said to [Peter] the third time, "Simon, son of Jonah, do you love Me?"

Peter was grieved because He said to him the third time, "Do you love Me?" And he said to Him, "Lord, You know all things; You know that I love You."

Jesus said to him, "Feed My sheep. Most assuredly, I say to you, when you were younger, you girded yourself and walked where you wished; but when you are old, you will stretch out your hands, and another will gird you and carry you where you do not wish." This He spoke, signifying by what death he would glorify God.

—JOHN 21:17–19

Now when they saw the boldness of Peter and John, and perceived that they were uneducated and untrained men, they marveled. And they realized that they had been with Jesus.

—ACTS 4:13

Building Endurance

■ *Called to Keep Growing*

"Listen! Behold, a sower went out to sow. And it happened, as he sowed, that some seed fell by the wayside; and the birds of the air came and devoured it. Some fell on stony ground, where it did not have much earth; and immediately it sprang up because it had no depth of earth.

But when the sun was up it was scorched, and because it had no root it withered away. And some seed fell among thorns; and the thorns grew up and choked it, and it yielded no crop. But other seed fell on good ground and yielded a crop that sprang up, increased and produced: some thirty-fold, some sixty, and some a hundred."

—MARK 4:3–8

[Be] confident of this very thing, that He who has begun a good work in you will complete it until the day of Jesus Christ.

—PHILIPPIANS 1:6

Nevertheless, to the degree that we have already attained, let us walk by the same rule, let us be of the same mind.

—PHILIPPIANS 3:16

For this reason I also suffer these things; nevertheless I am not ashamed, for I know whom I have believed and am persuaded that He is able to keep what I have committed to Him until that Day.

—2 TIMOTHY 1:12

■ Called to Overcome

"He who has an ear, let him hear what the Spirit says to the churches. To him who overcomes I will give to eat from the tree of life, which is in the midst of the Paradise of God. He who has an ear, let him hear what the Spirit says to the churches. To him who overcomes I will give some of the hidden manna to eat. And I will give him a white stone, and on the stone a new name written which no one knows except him who receives it.

"But hold fast what you have till I come. And he who overcomes, and keeps My works until the end, to him I will give power over the nations—

'He shall rule them with a rod of iron;
As the potter's vessels shall be broken to
     pieces'—
as I also have received from My Father; and I
     will give him the morning star."
—REVELATION 2:7,17,25-28

"He who overcomes shall be clothed in white garments, and I will not blot out his name from the Book of Life; but I will confess his name before My Father and before His angels. Behold, I come quickly! Hold fast what you have, that no one may take your crown. He who overcomes, I will make him a pillar in the temple of My God, and he shall go out no more. And I will write on him the name of My God and the name of the city of My God, the New Jerusalem, which comes down out of heaven from My God. And I will write on him My new name.

To him who overcomes I will grant to sit with Me on My throne, as I also overcame and sat down with My Father on His throne."

—REVELATION 3:5,11,12,21

"He who overcomes shall inherit all things, and I will be his God and he shall be My son."

—REVELATION 21:7

■ Called to Follow Through

"And whoever does not bear his cross and come after Me cannot be My disciple.

"For which of you, intending to build a tower, does not sit down first and count the cost, whether he has enough to finish it—lest, after he has laid the foundation, and is not able to finish it, all who see it begin to mock him, saying, 'This man began to build and was not able to finish.'

"Or what king, going to make war against another king, does not sit down first and consider whether he is able with ten thousand to meet him who comes against him with twenty thousand? Or else, while the other is still a great way off, he sends a delegation and asks conditions of peace. So likewise, whoever of you does not forsake all that he has cannot be My disciple.

"Salt is good; but if the salt has lost its flavor, how shall it be seasoned? It is neither fit for the land nor for the dunghill, but men throw it out. He who has ears to hear, let him hear!"

—LUKE 14:27–35

Making the Right Choices

"I call heaven and earth as witnesses today against you, that I have set before you life and death, blessing and cursing; therefore choose life, that both you and your descendants may live."

—DEUTERONOMY 30:19

So David said to God, "I have sinned greatly, because I have done this thing; but now, I pray, take away the iniquity of Your servant, for I have done very foolishly."

And the LORD spoke to Gad, David's seer, saying, "Go and tell David, saying, 'Thus says the LORD: "I offer you three things; choose one of them for yourself, that I may do it to you."'"

So Gad came to David and said to him, "Thus says the LORD: 'Choose for yourself, either three years of famine, or three months to be defeated by your foes with the sword of your enemies overtaking you, or else for three days the sword of the LORD—the plague in the land, with the angel of the LORD destroying throughout all the territory of Israel.' Now consider what answer I should take back to Him who sent me."

And David said to Gad, "I am in great distress. Please let me fall into the hand of the LORD, for His mercies are very great; but do not let me fall into the hand of man."

—1 CHRONICLES 21:8–13

"And if it seems evil to you to serve the LORD, choose for yourselves this day whom you will serve, whether the gods which your fathers served that were on the other side of the River, or the gods of the Amorites, in whose land you dwell. But as for me and my house, we will serve the LORD."

—JOSHUA 24:15

Receiving the Reward for Endurance

For no other foundation can anyone lay than that which is laid, which is Jesus Christ. Now if anyone builds on this foundation with gold, silver, precious stones, wood, hay, straw, each one's work will become manifest; for the Day will declare it, because it will be revealed by fire; and the fire will test each one's work, of what sort it is. If anyone's work which he has built on it endures, he will receive a reward.

—1 CORINTHIANS 3:11-14

Therefore do not cast away your confidence, which has great reward. For you have need of endurance, so that after you have done the will of God, you may receive the promise:

"For yet a little while,
And He who is coming will come and will not
    tarry.
Now the just shall live by faith;
But if anyone draws back,
My soul has no pleasure in him."

—HEBREWS 10:35-38

Look to yourselves, that we do not lose those things we worked for, but that we may receive a full reward.

—2 JOHN 1:8

[He] is able to keep you from stumbling,
And to present you faultless
Before the presence of His glory with
    exceeding joy.

—JUDE 1:24

CHAPTER 11

Finding "Fullness" in God

Scott Peck said it best in the very first sentence of his book, *The Road Less Traveled*: "Life is difficult." If we expect it to be any different, we've set ourselves up for continuous disappointment. Even if I am a Christian believer, I recognize that I am not home yet (in Heaven); therefore, my sojourn here on earth is imperfect and never fully satisfying or secure.

However, since we have been promised significant joy, and even some ecstasy in our lives, the challenge is in deciding where to go for those satisfactions. The call of the Scriptures is to turn to the things of God (not the refrigerator!) for fulfillment on this earth because they are a prelude to eternal bliss. We can taste everlasting life through reading God's Word, prayer, worship, and communion. "And God will wipe away every tear from their eyes; there shall be no more death, nor sorrow, nor crying; and there shall be no more pain" (Rev. 21:4).

Finding Satisfaction in God's Food

The poor shall eat and be satisfied;
Those who seek Him will praise the LORD.
Let your heart live forever!
All the prosperous of the earth
Shall eat and worship;
All those who go down to the dust
Shall bow before Him,
Even he who cannot keep himself alive.
                                        —PSALM 22:26,29

Bless the LORD, O my soul,
And forget not all His benefits:
Who forgives all your iniquities,
Who heals all your diseases,
Who redeems your life from destruction,
Who crowns you with lovingkindness and
    tender mercies,
Who satisfies your mouth with good things,
So that your youth is renewed like the eagle's.
                                        —PSALM 103:2–5

"Come, eat of my bread
And drink of the wine I have mixed."
—PROVERBS 9:5

"Ho! Everyone who thirsts,
Come to the waters;
And you who have no money,
Come, buy and eat.
Yes, come, buy wine and milk
Without money and without price.
Why do you spend money for what is not
    bread,
And your wages for what does not satisfy?
Listen diligently to Me, and eat what is good,
And let your soul delight itself in abundance."
—ISAIAH 55:1-2

"You shall eat in plenty and be satisfied,
And praise the name of the LORD your God,
Who has dealt wondrously with you;
And My people shall never be put to shame."
—JOEL 2:26

Now when one of those who sat at the table with Him heard these things, he said to Him, "Blessed is he who shall eat bread in the kingdom of God!"
—LUKE 14:15

For this reason I bow my knees to the Father of our Lord Jesus Christ, from whom the whole family in heaven and earth is named, that He would grant you, according to the riches of His glory, to be strengthened with might through His Spirit in the inner man, that Christ may dwell in your hearts through faith; that you, being rooted and grounded in love, may be able to comprehend with all the saints what is the width and length and depth and height—to know the love of Christ which passes knowledge; that you may be filled with all the fullness of God.

—EPHESIANS 3:14–19

Finding Satisfaction in Scripture Reading

Blessed is the man
Who walks not in the counsel of the ungodly,
Nor stands in the path of sinners,
Nor sits in the seat of the scornful;
But his delight is in the law of the LORD,
And in His law he meditates day and night.
He shall be like a tree
Planted by the rivers of water,
That brings forth its fruit in its season,
Whose leaf also shall not wither;
And whatever he does shall prosper.

—PSALM 1:1–3

Your word I have hidden in my heart,
That I might not sin against You!
I will delight myself in Your statutes;
I will not forget Your word.
So shall I have an answer for him who
 reproaches me,
For I trust in Your word.
This is my comfort in my affliction,
For Your word has given me life.
Your word is a lamp to my feet
And a light to my path.

—PSALM 119:11,16,42,50,105

All Scripture is given by inspiration of God, and is profitable for doctrine, for reproof, for correction, for instruction in righteousness, that the man of God may be complete, thoroughly equipped for every good work.

—2 TIMOTHY 3:16–17

Finding Satisfaction in Prayer

Then He said to them, "Why do you sleep? Rise and pray, lest you enter into temptation."

—LUKE 22:46

Likewise the Spirit also helps in our weaknesses. For we do not know what we should pray for as we ought, but the Spirit Himself makes intercession for us with groanings which cannot be uttered. Now He who searches the hearts knows what the mind of the Spirit is, because He makes intercession for the saints according to the will of God. And we know that all things work together for good to those who love God, to those who are the called according to His purpose.

—ROMANS 8:26–28

Be anxious for nothing, but in everything by prayer and supplication, with thanksgiving, let your requests be made known to God.

—PHILIPPIANS 4:6

Pray without ceasing.

—1 THESSALONIANS 5:17

Therefore I exhort first of all that supplications, prayers, intercessions, and giving of thanks be made for all men. I desire therefore that the men pray everywhere, lifting up holy hands, without wrath and doubting.

—1 TIMOTHY 2:1,8

Is anyone among you suffering? Let him pray. Is anyone cheerful? Let him sing psalms. Is anyone among you sick? Let him call for the elders of the church, and let them pray over him, anointing him with oil in the name of the Lord. And the prayer of faith will save the sick, and the Lord will raise him up. And if he has committed sins, he will be forgiven.

Confess your trespasses to one another, and pray for one another, that you may be healed. The effective, fervent prayer of a righteous man avails much.

Elijah was a man with a nature like ours, and he prayed earnestly that it would not rain; and it did not rain on the land for three years and six months. And he prayed again, and the heaven gave rain, and the earth produced its fruit.

—JAMES 5:13-18

Therefore by Him let us continually offer the sacrifice of praise to God, that is, the fruit of our lips, giving thanks to His name.

—HEBREWS 13:15

"For the eyes of the LORD are on the
   righteous,
And His ears are open to their prayers;
But the face of the LORD is against those who
   do evil."

—1 PETER 3:12

But the end of all things is at hand; therefore be serious and watchful in your prayers.

—1 PETER 4:7

Finding Satisfaction in Worship

Oh, give thanks to the LORD!
Call upon His name;
Make known His deeds among the peoples!
Sing to Him, sing psalms to Him;
Talk of all His wondrous works!
Glory in His holy name;
Let the hearts of those rejoice who seek the LORD!
Seek the LORD and His strength;
Seek His face evermore!

—PSALM 105:1-4

Jesus said to her, "Woman, believe Me, the hour is coming when you will neither on this mountain, nor in Jerusalem, worship the Father. You worship what you do not know; we know what we worship, for salvation is of the Jews.

But the hour is coming, and now is, when the true worshipers will worship the Father in spirit and truth; for the Father is seeking such to worship Him. God is Spirit, and those who worship Him must worship in spirit and truth."

—JOHN 4:21-24

The twenty-four elders fall down before Him who sits on the throne and worship Him who lives forever and ever, and cast their crowns before the throne.

—REVELATION 4:10

"Fear God and give glory to Him, for the hour of His judgment has come; and worship Him who made heaven and earth, the sea and springs of water."

—REVELATION 14:7

"Who shall not fear You, O Lord, and glorify Your name?
For You alone are holy.
For all nations shall come and worship before You,
For Your judgments have been manifested."

—REVELATION 15:4

Finding Satisfaction in Doing Good

And let us not grow weary while doing good, for in due season we shall reap if we do not lose heart. Therefore, as we have opportunity, let us do good to all, especially to those who are of the household of faith.

—GALATIANS 6:9

But be doers of the word, and not hearers only, deceiving yourselves. For if anyone is a hearer of the word and not a doer, he is like a man observing his natural face in a mirror; for he observes himself, goes away, and immediately forgets what kind of man he was. But he who looks into the perfect law of liberty and continues in it, and is not a forgetful hearer but a doer of the work, this one will be blessed in what he does.

—JAMES 1:22-25

Pure and undefiled religion before God and the Father is this: to visit orphans and widows in their trouble, and to keep oneself unspotted from the world.

—JAMES 1:27

Finding Satisfaction in Complete Dedication

For to me, to live is Christ, and to die is gain.

—PHILIPPIANS 1:21

But what things were gain to me, these I have counted loss for Christ. But indeed I also count all things loss for the excellence of the knowledge of Christ Jesus my Lord, for whom I have suffered the loss of all things, and count them as rubbish, that I may gain Christ and be found in Him, not having my own righteousness, which is from the law, but that which is through faith in Christ, the righteousness which is from God by faith; that I may know Him and the power of His resurrection, and the fellowship of His sufferings, being conformed to His death, if, by any means, I may attain to the resurrection from the dead.

Not that I have already attained, or am already perfected; but I press on, that I may lay hold of that for which Christ Jesus has also laid hold of me. Brethren, I do not count myself to have apprehended; but one thing I do, forgetting those things which are behind and reaching forward to those things which are ahead, I press toward the goal for the prize of the upward call of God in Christ Jesus.

—PHILIPPIANS 3:7–14

As you have therefore received Christ Jesus the Lord, so walk in Him, rooted and built up in Him and established in the faith, as you have been taught, abounding in it with thanksgiving. Beware lest anyone cheat you through philosophy and empty deceit, according to the tradition of men, according to the basic principles of the world, and not according to Christ. For in Him dwells all the fullness of the Godhead bodily; and you are complete in Him, who is the head of all principality and power.

—COLOSSIANS 2:6–10

Finding Satisfaction in Christ, Food for the Soul

And as they were eating, Jesus took bread, blessed it and broke it, and gave it to the disciples and said, "Take, eat; this is My body." Then He took the cup, and gave thanks, and gave it to them, saying, "Drink from it, all of you.

For this is My blood of the new covenant, which is shed for many for the remission of sins."

—MATTHEW 26:26–28

"Do not labor for the food which perishes, but for the food which endures to everlasting life, which the Son of Man will give you, because God the Father has set His seal on Him."

—JOHN 6:27

Then Jesus said to them, "Most assuredly, I say to you, Moses did not give you the bread from heaven, but My Father gives you the true bread from heaven. For the bread of God is He who comes down from heaven and gives life to the world."

Then they said to Him, "Lord, give us this bread always."

And Jesus said to them, "I am the bread of life. He who comes to Me shall never hunger, and he who believes in Me shall never thirst.

"I am the living bread which came down from heaven. If anyone eats of this bread, he will live forever; and the bread that I shall give is My flesh, which I shall give for the life of the world."

The Jews therefore quarreled among themselves, saying, "How can this Man give us His flesh to eat?"

Then Jesus said to them, "Most assuredly, I say to you, unless you eat the flesh of the Son of Man and drink His blood, you have no life in you. Whoever eats My flesh and drinks My blood has eternal life, and I will raise him up at the last day. For My flesh is food indeed, and My blood is drink indeed. He who eats My flesh and drinks My blood abides in Me, and I in him. As the living Father sent Me, and I live because of the Father, so he who feeds on Me will live because of Me. This is the bread which came down from heaven—not as your fathers ate the manna, and are dead. He who eats this bread will live forever."

—JOHN 6:32–35, 51–58

For as often as you eat this bread and drink this cup, you proclaim the Lord's death till He comes.
—1 CORINTHIANS 11:26

Carrying the Recovery Message to Others

Jesus said it to a man He had just healed: Go home and tell about God's goodness to you.

What about you? Have you experienced some healing? How did it happen? Was it all your doing? Or can you give a word of recommendation to your Higher Power?

"You can't keep it unless you give it away." The ultimate paradox! Yet we know it's true. Ultimately, we want happiness. But we know it will only come when we release our white-knuckled grasp on what we think will get it for us (name your addiction here: _____) and turn our attention to making the lives of others a little more happy.

Thanking God for My Own 'Spiritual Awakening'

It is good to give thanks to the LORD,
And to sing praises to Your name, O Most
   High;
To declare Your lovingkindness in the
   morning,
And Your faithfulness every night,
On an instrument of ten strings,
On the lute,
And on the harp,
With harmonious sound.
For You, LORD, have made me glad through
   Your work;
I will triumph in the works of Your hands.

—PSALM 92:1–4

Oh, sing to the LORD a new song!
Sing to the LORD, all the earth.
Sing to the LORD, bless His name;
Proclaim the good news of His salvation from
   day to day.

—PSALM 96:1–2

Praise the LORD!
Oh, give thanks to the LORD, for He is good!
For His mercy endures forever.

Who can utter the mighty acts of the LORD?
Or can declare all His praise?
Blessed are those who keep justice,
And he who does righteousness at all times!

—PSALM 106:1–3

Oh, give thanks to the LORD, for He is good!
For His mercy endures forever.
Let the redeemed of the LORD say so,
Whom He has redeemed from the hand of the
enemy.

—PSALM 107:1–2

Oh, that men would give thanks to the LORD
for His goodness,
And for His wonderful works to the children
of men!
Let them sacrifice the sacrifices of
thanksgiving,
And declare His works with rejoicing.

—PSALM 107:21–22

And I thank Christ Jesus our Lord who has en-
abled me, because He counted me faithful, putting me into the ministry, although I was formerly
a blasphemer, a persecutor, and an insolent man;
but I obtained mercy because I did it ignorantly in
unbelief. And the grace of our Lord was exceedingly abundant, with faith and love which are in

Christ Jesus. This is a faithful saying and worthy of all acceptance, that Christ Jesus came into the world to save sinners, of whom I am chief. However, for this reason I obtained mercy, that in me first Jesus Christ might show all longsuffering, as a pattern to those who are going to believe on Him for everlasting life.

—1 TIMOTHY 1:12–16

Offering the New Life to Others, Through My 'Walk'

"Let your light so shine before men, that they may see your good works and glorify your Father in heaven."

—MATTHEW 5:16

To the weak I became as weak, that I might win the weak. I have become all things to all men, that I might by all means save some. Now this I do for the gospel's sake, that I may be partaker of it with you. Do you not know that those who run in a race all run, but one receives the prize? Run in such a way that you may obtain it.

And everyone who competes for the prize is temperate in all things. Now they do it to obtain a perishable crown, but we for an imperishable crown. Therefore I run thus: not with uncertainty. Thus I fight: not as one who beats the air. But I discipline my body and bring it into subjection, lest, when I have preached to others, I myself should become disqualified.

—1 CORINTHIANS 9:22–27

Now thanks be to God who always leads us in triumph in Christ, and through us diffuses the fragrance of His knowledge in every place. For we are to God the fragrance of Christ among those who are being saved and among those who are perishing. To the one we are the aroma of death leading to death, and to the other the aroma of life to life. And who is sufficient for these things? For we are not, as so many, peddling the word of God; but as of sincerity, but as from God, we speak in the sight of God in Christ.

—2 CORINTHIANS 2:14–17

For this reason we also, since the day we heard it, do not cease to pray for you, and to ask that you may be filled with the knowledge of His will in all wisdom and spiritual understanding; that you may walk worthy of the Lord, fully pleasing Him, being fruitful in every good work and increasing in the knowledge of God; strengthened with all might, according to His glorious power, for all patience and longsuffering with joy; giving thanks to the Father who has qualified us to be partakers of the inheritance of the saints in the light.

—COLOSSIANS 1:9–12

For you were once darkness, but now you are light in the Lord. Walk as children of light (for the fruit of the Spirit is in all goodness, righteousness, and truth), proving what is acceptable to the Lord.

—EPHESIANS 5:8–10

Offering the New Life to Others, Through My Words

Now all things are of God, who has reconciled us to Himself through Jesus Christ, and has given us the ministry of reconciliation, that is, that God was in Christ reconciling the world to Himself, not imputing their trespasses to them, and has committed to us the word of reconciliation. Therefore we are ambassadors for Christ, as though God were pleading through us: we implore you on Christ's behalf, be reconciled to God.

—2 CORINTHIANS 5:18–20

Then the eleven disciples went away into Galilee, to the mountain which Jesus had appointed for them. And when they saw Him, they worshiped Him; but some doubted.

Then Jesus came and spoke to them, saying,

"All authority has been given to Me in heaven and on earth. Go therefore and make disciples of all the nations, baptizing them in the name of the Father and of the Son and of the Holy Spirit, teaching them to observe all things that I have commanded you; and lo, I am with you always, even to the end of the age." Amen.

—MATTHEW 28:16–20

"But you shall receive power when the Holy Spirit has come upon you; and you shall be witnesses to Me in Jerusalem, and in all Judea and Samaria, and to the end of the earth."

—ACTS 1:8

To them God willed to make known what are the riches of the glory of this mystery among the Gentiles: which is Christ in you, the hope of glory. Him we preach, warning every man and teaching every man in all wisdom, that we may present every man perfect in Christ Jesus. To this end I also labor, striving according to His working which works in me mightily.

—COLOSSIANS 1:27–29

Index

Old Testament

New Testament